D1611535

WITHDRAWN

Carter G. Woodson Institute

Series in Black Studies

ARMSTEAD L. ROBINSON, *Editor*

Enterprising Southerners

BLACK ECONOMIC SUCCESS IN NORTH CAROLINA,
1865 – 1915

Robert C. Kenzer

University Press of Virginia

Charlottesville & London

Portions of chapter 2 appeared in Robert C. Kenzer, "The Black Businessman in the Postwar South: North Carolina, 1865–1880," *Business History Review,* summer 1989. Copyright © 1989 by the President and Fellows of Harvard College. Reprinted by permission of Harvard Business School.

THE UNIVERSITY PRESS OF VIRGINIA
© 1997 by the Rector and Visitors
of the University of Virginia
All rights reserved
Printed in the United States of America

First published 1997

∞ The paper used in this publication meets the minimum requirements of the American National Standard for Information Sciences—Permanence of Paper for Printed Library Materials, ANSI Z39.48-1984.

Library of Congress Cataloging-in-Publication Data

Kenzer, Robert C., 1955–
  Enterprising southerners : Black economic success in North Carolina, 1865–1915 / Robert C. Kenzer.
      p.   cm. — (Carter G. Woodson Institute series in Black studies)
    Includes bibliographical references and index.
    ISBN 0-8139-1733-6 (cloth : alk. paper)
      1. Afro-Americans—North Carolina—Economic conditions.   2. Afro-Americans—1863–1877.   3. Afro-Americans—1877–1864.   4. North Carolina—Economic conditions.   I. Title.   II. Series.
  E185.93.N6K46   1997   97-2295
  330.9756'041'08996073—dc21   CIP

For my son, Benjamin

Contents

Illustrations

Tables

Preface

THIS STUDY of black economic success in North Carolina began fifteen years ago when I was making some last-minute revisions on my doctoral dissertation, an examination of the impact of the Civil War on community and family life in Orange County, North Carolina. While my dissertation focused largely on the war's effect on whites, I had copied all the statistical information provided by the manuscript census on the community's black residents. I decided that it would be interesting to compare the economic status of the county's mulattoes with that of its blacks in 1870. I found that the mulattoes were twice as likely as blacks to own real estate. Intrigued by this finding, I proceeded to compare occupations. I discovered that the mulattoes also were twice as likely as blacks to have a blue-collar skill.

After finishing my dissertation, I decided to follow up my findings on the economic status of blacks and mulattoes in Orange County by examining their status in the other North Carolina counties. After analyzing the more than 60,000 households headed by African-American men in the state, I found that, with very few exceptions, in nearly every county the economic status of mulattoes was well above that of blacks. In fact, in 1870 mulattoes statewide were nearly four times as likely as blacks to own real estate.

In order to explain the difference between these two groups, I began to examine every page of the 1860 manuscript census to find how many of the postwar African-American landowners had been free in 1860 and

how many owned property at that point in time. Although this task
proved to be even more difficult than tracing the 1870 manuscript census, I continually was rewarded with the excitement of discovering that
many of those who owned land in 1870 also owned land in 1860. Further, I began to feel that there was enough material on African Americans who experienced economic success and the comparative status of
blacks and mulattoes to write an entire book on the subject.

I was further convinced that this topic was worthy of a book-length
study after I finished copying all of the credit ratings of North Carolina
black businessmen. These entrepreneurs, or "enterprising" men, as they
often were called in both credit ratings and newspapers, like postbellum
black landowners, were disproportionately mulattoes who had experienced antebellum freedom.

A chance encounter with a document in the Charles N. Hunter Collection, the largest set of papers concerning blacks in the Special Collections Library of Duke University, led me to rethink the scope of the study
I was envisioning. This document was a questionnaire that George Allen
Mebane, a leading black North Carolinian, used to compile information
on prominent black North Carolinians from 1860 to 1885. Mebane
planned to use this questionnaire as the foundation for a book on this
topic. In his questionnaire Mebane made it clear that although his book
was to be a study of blacks who were economically successful, what interested him was the environment in which these individuals achieved their
success. He was as intrigued by politics and other forces at work in the
black community as he was by economics. When I discovered that Mebane was a politician as well as a storekeeper, teacher, and editor, I began
to realize why he was interested in the environment that allowed some
blacks to experience economic success.

In addition to deciding to broaden the scope of my study beyond economics, I also began to consider expanding its chronological span well
beyond the immediate postwar years. My decision to trace my topic up
to 1915 was based partly on two sources that had not been used by previous historians. First, after the turn of the century the state tax commissioner of North Carolina began to compile very detailed records on the
amount of property blacks owned in every county, and these records
were kept through 1915. Second, although black-operated newspapers
were published earlier, it was not until the 1890s that they began to be
preserved on a wide enough scale to reveal important aspects of black
economic success. This was particularly true of one of the leading black
newspapers, *Star of Zion*.

A 3-month research trip to North Carolina during the fall of 1988 led
me to consider extending the time span of my study into the early twen-

tieth century. While I was in North Carolina I decided to follow up the suggestion of John Hope Franklin that I contact one of his former graduate students, Loren Schweninger, who was teaching in Greensboro and writing a history of black property owners in the South from 1790 to 1915. After meeting Schweninger and learning more about his work, I became convinced of the merits of ending my own study in 1915 as well. In Chapel Hill, George Tindall and Joel Williamson, both of whom had examined postwar southern blacks and had had to decide where to stop, persuaded me of the value of taking my study up to 1915.

My debt goes beyond those scholars who influenced the chronological scope of this book. My research was generously funded by the Department of History and the College of Family, Home, and Social Science of Brigham Young University, an Archie K. Davis Fellowship from the North Caroliniana Society, a Donald B. Hoffman Faculty Research Award from Phi Alpha Theta, and an Albert J. Beveridge Grant for Research from the American Historical Association.

A number of archives and their staffs were especially helpful. Of particular note are the Southern Historical Collection and the North Carolina Collection of the University of North Carolina at Chapel Hill, the Special Collections Library of Duke University, the East Carolina University Archives, the North Carolina State Archives, and the Cape Fear Museum in Wilmington. I am especially indebted to the Prince Hall Grand Lodge Free and Accepted Masons of North Carolina for allowing me to copy their membership lists in the state Grand Lodge office and for introducing me to a number of local lodges whose records proved to be particularly rich.

I am grateful to three former colleagues at Brigham Young University who commented on various drafts of chapters: Rodney Bohac, Martha Bradley, and Mary Stovall Richards. I am also obliged to three University of Richmond colleagues who have been particularly supportive during the process of finding a publisher for my study: John L. Gordon, John D. Treadway, and R. Barry Westin. Although there is not room to list their specific contributions, I would like to thank a number of other individuals without whom I would never have been able to complete my research and writing: Anne Berkley, W. Fitzhugh Brundage, R. Kelly Bryant Jr., William A. Clement, Raymond Gavins, Glenda Gilmore, Michael Hill, James Leloudis, Stephen E. Massengill, Kirsten Mullin, William C. Parker Jr., William S. Powell, J. C. Scarborough III, and Barnetta White. Further, I must thank Deborah Govoruhk, secretary of the University of Richmond history department, for helping me prepare the manuscript. Appreciation is also due to the University Press of Virginia and particularly to Richard Holway for his constant guidance and patience.

My greatest obligation, as always, is to my wife, Carol, who over many years has patiently listened as I voiced my many concerns about how the research and writing of the book was progressing, provided valuable criticism on various aspects of the manuscript, and, most importantly, constantly encouraged me to see the study through to its conclusion.

Finally, I want to acknowledge two individuals who died at much too young an age while I was working on this book: my brother Ron, who prompted my interest in economic and business history and who was fascinated by why certain people were successful; and Armstead L. Robinson, who encouraged me to submit my manuscript to the University Press of Virginia and provided invaluable suggestions for improving it.

Introduction

IN 1885 George Allen Mebane, a black newspaper editor, proposed writing a 300-page book called "The Prominent Colored Men of North Carolina."[1] This book would document what Mebane termed "the progress of the race" from 1860 to 1885 and would include biographical sketches of 200 of the state's leading black businessmen and politicians as well as provide a description and history of those institutions in the state that aided blacks. Mebane even went so far as to send out a detailed questionnaire to those who would be the subjects of these biographical sketches in order to find out whether their parents had been freedmen or slaves before the war, the extent of their schooling, their occupations, and the amount of property they owned.

Mebane himself clearly fit these criteria for designation as "a prominent colored" man of North Carolina during the postslavery era. He was born on 4 July 1850, at Hermitage, in Bertie County, North Carolina, to slave parents. Nothing is known about his early life except that by the latter part of 1864 his parents had fled to McKean County, Pennsylvania, and shortly thereafter he served in the Civil War as a mess boy in Company A, 85th New York Regiment of Volunteers. After the war Mebane returned to North Carolina, where over the course of four decades he taught, was elected as a Republican state senator for two terms, edited the black-owned *Carolina Enterprise,* maintained a provisions store, and acted as an incorporator, financial agent, and general superintendent of the Elizabeth City Colored Normal and Industrial Institute. At the turn

1. George Allen Mebane. (Courtesy of North
Carolina Division of Archives and History,
N79.4.4)

of the century Mebane also authored two insightful article-length studies
on race.

Perhaps in part because of his many different pursuits, Mebane never
completed his study of prominent black North Carolinians. Nevertheless, that Mebane asked his subjects not just to provide specific details of
their lives but also to include "general remarks and incidents in [their]
life" suggests that he wanted to gain some sense of why these individuals
felt they had achieved their success despite the general adversity they
and their race had encountered under slavery and since emancipation.

This study of black economic success in North Carolina from 1865 to
1915 attempts to address many of the same issues George Allen Mebane
raised more than a century ago. Like Mebane, it also reaches back to the
period before general emancipation to determine the degree to which
antebellum status influenced the success blacks from different backgrounds experienced in the post-war South. Also like Mebane, in addition to describing who experienced financial success, it examines the
social and political forces that shaped that success.

AN IMPORTANT WORK!!

The writer proposes, and has in course of preparation, a book to be known as

"The Prominent Colored Men
OF
NORTH CAROLINA,"
FROM 1860 TO 1885 INCLUSIVE.

This will include a period of twenty-five years, or two and one-half decades. The work will contain a succinct biographical sketch of over two hundred prominent colored business men and politicians together with a description and history of all the institutions in the State, erected for the especial benefit of the colored people,

It is the object of the author to have the work replete with regard to data and statistics, regarding the progress of the race—intellectually and financially. It will contain about three hundred pages and will be put in market about the first of September.

Any information furnished by you will be duly credited and thankfully received

Yours respectfully, &c.,

G. A. MEBANE.

1. Name ....
2. Residence, ...
3. When and where born, ...
4. Of slave or free parentage, ...
5. Attended what schools and how long, ...

....

6. Occupation, ...
7. No acres land owned, ...
8. Total value property, ...
9. Greatest quantity of produce raised in any one year ....

....

10. No. of copies subscribed for, ...
11. Amount to be paid when notice is given that the work is in press,

....

General remarks and incidents in life:— ....

....

....

....

....

....

....

2. Mebane Questionnaire. (Courtesy of Special Collections Library, Duke University, Charles N. Hunter Papers)

The present study goes well beyond an examination of 200 individuals. Indeed, whenever possible, it attempts to consider every black who owned land and ran a business both in particular communities and, sometimes, in the entire state. Further, rather than stopping in 1885, it traces the nature of black economic success as late as 50 years after the Civil War. It thus embraces a major historical era whose parameters Mebane could not have considered when he proposed his book in 1885.

During his lifetime George Mebane was not the only black who was interested in chronicling the successes of the freedom generation of black Americans to which he belonged—slaves and their children who were freed by the Civil War.[2] Another former slave who lived through this era, Booker T. Washington, also was preoccupied with explaining how blacks were adjusting after 1865 to their heritage of slavery. Like Mebane, Washington felt that it was essential to reveal to whites as well as members of his own race that although most freedmen were encountering difficulties, clearly a significant minority of blacks were experiencing improving conditions of development, particularly in the economic sphere. Washington actively publicized the efforts of black entrepreneurs through the National Negro Business League, which he formed in 1900, as well as through his very visible promotion of the efforts of various black business communities, most notably Durham, North Carolina.[3]

Washington's efforts were paralleled by those of the black scholar and social critic W. E. B. Du Bois, whose series of studies at Atlanta University at the turn of the century documented the success blacks experienced not only in initiating business but also in creating a social and cultural infrastructure. Despite these accomplishments, Du Bois expressed concern about the impact of the heritage of slavery and the impediments racism placed in the path of former slaves.[4]

Although he followed in Washington's and Du Bois's footsteps in studying the progress of blacks since emancipation, the black sociologist E. Franklin Frazier clearly was not a contemporary observer of the freedom generation. And by the time Frazier began to publish his major works, during the 1930s and 1940s, a sizable share of blacks, most of whom had not known slavery firsthand, had left the South and migrated to the urban North. Nevertheless, Frazier, like Washington and Du Bois, was interested in how the heritage of slavery influenced blacks. He portrayed its legacy in very negative terms for three reasons: one, born in the 1890s, he did not witness firsthand the gains of the freedom generation; two, the rate of racial progress seemed to slow in the early twentieth century; and three, the detrimental impact of urbanization seemed so pervasive.[5]

While Frazier's linkage between the heritage of slavery and the lack of achievement of the descendants of slaves had its fullest impact years later, when it shaped the Moynihan Report of 1965, it was Stanley M. Elkins's *Slavery: A Problem of American Institutional and Intellectual Life* (1959) that altered the debate among historians about the extent to which slavery impeded black post-emancipation development.[6] Elkins's portrayal of the detrimental impact of slavery on personality was so striking that it forced a reconsideration of the nature of the institution. The result was a series of revisionist works during the 1970s by John W. Blassingame, Eugene D. Genovese, Robert W. Fogel and Stanley L. Engerman, and Herbert F. Gutman.[7] While these studies used varying methodologies and sources, all concluded that the detrimental impact of slavery was not as great as Frazier and Elkins had portrayed it to be. As Peter Kolchin has noted in analyzing these revisionist works, all agree that slaves "in many ways were able to help shape their own lives."[8]

If there was general agreement during the 1970s that the heritage of slavery did not limit the capacity of blacks to establish successful patterns of development after the Civil War, there was still the question to what degree diminished black economic opportunity in the postwar South resulted from either flawed regional infrastructure or racial prejudice. As economists and economic historians focused their attention on this issue in the late 1970s and into the 1980s, they came to remarkably varying and conflicting interpretations. While some emphasized the role of free market forces, others underscored the legacy of slavery and racism. While some concluded that black opportunity was shaped largely by the impact of international forces on the southern economy, others thought that black misfortunes were determined by distinctly southern factors, including the continuing influence of the plantation system.[9]

It was in reaction not to their differing conclusions but to six common shortcomings of these analytical frameworks that the present study of black economic success in North Carolina was initiated. First, while all agree that most blacks did not experience substantial economic gains during this era, they fail to explain how and why a significant minority did acquire land and conduct businesses. Second, none of the studies define what would have constituted a satisfactory economic gain for blacks. In other words, they provide no benchmark of success to use in judging how far short blacks fell. Would we expect any group of newly arrived immigrants in the immediate postwar South who lacked property and were largely illiterate to acquire within fifty years an economic status matching that of the prewar property owners of the region? Third, all of these studies view black Southerners in largely monolithic terms, ignoring evidence of differential rates of success based upon antebellum status and skin complexion. Fourth, since they focus primarily on quantitative economic indicators of the individual's level of success, none consider the role of family, community, collective identity, or politics. Fifth, because they rely on fragmentary databases, none suggest any variation by location within the region or within a single state. Sixth, none take an incremental approach to the topic by tracing short-term patterns (such as one year at a time) for an extended period of time.

This book addresses a number of these shortcomings. In chapter 1 I trace black landownership in North Carolina from 1865 to 1915. I begin by looking at the 4,000 black men who owned real estate just after the war to determine to what degree prewar emancipation and skin complexion corresponded with their ability to acquire land. Then, using available tax records and reports of the state tax commissioner, I trace county by county for the entire state blacks' slow but steady progress in acquiring real estate through 1915. I emphasize how the flexibility of the urban real-estate market rather than an absence of racism enhanced black landownership in cities more than in the countryside.

In chapter 2 I proceed to examine those blacks who conducted businesses in the state during the first fifty years of freedom. Using credit ratings and business directories, I determine which types of communities and regions of the state were conducive to black entrepreneurial success. I conclude that the economic opportunities of the black business community were not severely hindered either by the end of Reconstruction during the 1870s or by disfranchisement, which followed North Carolina's second Reconstruction, in the 1890s. Indeed, even in such cities as Wilmington, where one would expect to find that there was a severe decline in economic opportunity in the aftermath of the bloody race riot of 1898, black entrepreneurs experienced rates of success that equaled, and in some ways surpassed, those they had known previously.

In chapter 3 I investigate the role of black collective efforts toward enterprise throughout this era. Although I look at a number of examples of collective enterprise, by far the most important contribution to this topic is the detailed analysis of how black freemasonry assisted the black business community. Further, I describe how the National Negro Business League functioned at the local level.

Chapter 4, on the politics of enterprise, traces to what degree participation in politics at the state and local level aided the economic endeavors of blacks. I find that black landowners and businessmen who served in the state legislature or county and municipal government or held federal patronage posts were able to use their positions to enhance not just their own economic opportunities but also those of other blacks.

In chapter 5 I describe family, marriage, and education among black landholders and entrepreneurs. In addition to tracing the relationship between economic success and marriage partner, I use records from black colleges to examine the educational and professional careers of the children of economically successful blacks.

A number of valuable historical works have dealt with some of the topics included in these chapters. This study argues that prewar emancipation was an important factor in immediate postwar economic success for blacks, a finding that is compatible with John Hope Franklin's monumental work *The Free Negro in North Carolina, 1790–1860*. I pick up where Franklin ends chronologically but place much greater emphasis on differences between the experiences of blacks and mulattoes. August Meier's *Negro Thought in America, 1880–1915* provides an exceptional overview of the major black ideologies of this era, but his national scope makes it impossible to view how these ideas were put into action at the state or local level. Whereas Walter B. Weare's *Black Business in the New South* highlights the entrepreneurial talent and success of the most prominent black firm in North Carolina, perhaps in the entire nation, the present study examines black entrepreneurs who were engaged in all types of endeavors across the entire state, from the smallest hamlets to the largest cities. *Black Property Owners in the South, 1790–1915*, by Loren Schweninger, has a much broader chronological and geographic scope than this study; as a result, however, it does not go into the depth necessary to understand why particular communities provided distinctive opportunity for blacks, nor does it deal with such noneconomic issues as politics, marriage, and education. Willard B. Gatewood's *Aristocrats of Color* provides a valuable profile of the upper crust of black society. While my own study includes the type of individuals Gatewood describes, it also provides broader context for nonelite blacks, from whom many of the upper crust emerged. Finally, the major new synthesis of southern history for this era, Edward L. Ayers's *Promise of the New South*, deals with the varied experience of blacks during these years, but the shortage of local studies and the total absence of state studies of black economic opportunity limit his ability to generalize about patterns within the entire region, in subregions, or between states.

Since this study differentiates between blacks on the basis of complexion, a word about terminology is necessary. Throughout this book I use the word *black* when describing the collective experience of North Carolinians of African ancestry. However, often it is necessary to use the term *African American* when drawing distinctions between those who were denoted in census reports as being either black or mulatto. Clearly, these reports were based on subjective evaluations made overwhelmingly by white enumerators. Further, often an individual was not described in the same way from one census to the next. In such cases the individual is considered to be mulatto. For group measurements, unless otherwise specified, the census designation for the year under consideration was used. Despite their shortcomings, these designations are invaluable for distinguishing significant differences in patterns of economic opportunity.

Finally, some may wonder whether the story of black economic success in North Carolina is representative of the entire southern experience. As noted earlier, George Allen Mebane planned to write his history of prominent blacks in 1885, just twenty years after general emancipation. He could not foresee the unique circumstances in his native state that would alter the course of opportunity for these individuals and their descendants. North Carolina was exceptional among southern states in that it experienced a second political reconstruction during the 1890s. During that decade, largely through the support of black voters, the Republican Party in an alliance with the Populist Party gained control of local and state government and also elected a majority non-Democratic delegation to Congress. The Republican-Populist coalition rapidly reversed the political direction in which the Democrats had taken the state after they ended Reconstruction during the mid 1870s.[10]

Although black North Carolinians had reason to be especially optimistic about their political future during the 1890s, there is evidence that many felt equally confident about their personal future and their collective economic and social status. This study examines whether their optimism was justified given the second redemption the state witnessed, in which the Democrats used both the ballot box and violence to regain political power, which they quickly utilized to disfranchise most blacks. Hence, although North Carolina's political history is somewhat different from that of most southern states, that difference allows an examination of the degree to which black North Carolinians preserved the economic gains they had made after this second political reversal occurred.

A database allowing more accurate regional generalizations about the freedom generation will emerge as scholars conduct similar analyses of other southern states. Completion of these studies will bring scholars closer to a full understanding of the economic successes of the freedom generation, to which George Allen Mebane hoped to contribute when he began to compile his book on black North Carolinians in 1885.

1

Black Landownership

ON 26 DECEMBER 1865 in Warren County, North Carolina, William S. Williams became the owner of a 2-acre tract located in the town of Warrenton along the public road to Louisburg by paying $300 to Joseph J. Haithcock, the owner of the land.[1] When the deed completing this purchase was filed at the county courthouse, the white county registrar of deeds included the abbreviation "col." in parentheses after Williams's name, a common practice in recording land purchases by blacks. Who was William S. Williams and what might his purchase of 2 acres indicate about blacks' ability to buy land after the Civil War?

Before the Civil War Williams was a mulatto shoemaker.[2] Although exactly when he became free is not known, there is evidence that during the Civil War Williams earned enough money in his trade to buy his wife, Jane, out of bondage. One factor that may have assisted Williams financially was that he learned, according to a Warren County chronicler, "without a teacher, how to read and write and cipher without loss to himself."

By 1870 Williams had become a dry-goods merchant in Warrenton, the county seat, and the owner of land worth $1,150. Described by a white credit rater as a "remarkably cautious & economic" businessman, by 1877 Williams had made "$20,000 since the war" by diversification into butchering, transportation, and livery firms. According to one writer, Williams may eventually have accumulated the extraordinary sum of $50,000, which he invested in notes, bonds, and land. The great-

est tribute to his outstanding character and business habits came from a
white credit rater, who claimed in 1871 that he "would not be uneasy"
if Williams owed him $1,000.

Williams clearly was an exceptional individual whose economic advancement would have been considered remarkable even if he had been
white. While few black North Carolinians attained the level of landownership that Williams did, by 1870 nearly 4,000 others also owned real
estate, and thousands more would by 1915. It should be stressed that
these landowners never represented more than a very small share of the
entire black population in North Carolina and therefore in a sense were
nearly as exceptional as Williams. Nevertheless, understanding why certain individuals were able to acquire land will allow us to determine the
extent of blacks' economic opportunity in the postwar years. Significantly, the four factors that most enhanced blacks' chances of owning
land were all characteristics possessed by William S. Williams: being mulatto, experiencing antebellum freedom, having a nonagricultural occupation, and being an urban resident.

Whereas William S. Williams directly purchased his land, other Warren
County blacks used a variety of methods to acquire land during the mid
to late 1860s. Some even became landowners without spending any
money. For example, Haywood Williams, described in 1865 as "formerly
a slave, now a Freedman," was given 125 acres by Samuel A. Williams
"for and in consideration of the faithful manner in which the said Haywood has ever discharged all his duties towards the said Williams."[3]

Out of the same motivation that led Samuel Williams to give Haywood Williams land, but on slightly less generous terms, some masters
sold property to their former slaves for a nominal sum. Early in 1868
William J. Hawkins, of Warren County, sold to his former slave Indiana
Hawkins, the wife of Reuben Hawkins, a mulatto brickmason, 50 acres
for just $10 "on account of her fidelity and uniform kindness to her Mis-
tress and the children, the receipt of which is hereby acknowledged."[4]

Some former masters used a less direct route to transfer property to
their ex-slaves. These whites specified in their wills that after they died
their land should be sold to their former bondsmen. In 1869 Peter R.
Davis, the executor of the Hugh J. Davis estate in Warren sold 20 acres
for $140 to Henry Williams, a black, "by virtue of the powers conferred
to him in the will of Hugh J. Davis."[5]

In some cases blacks blocked from inheriting land from their former
masters sued in the courts. Hence, when Lewis Y. Christmas, a planter in
Warren, died and bequeathed $2,000 in land to his former slaves Chris-
topher, Erasmus, Marcus, and Keziah Christmas, his executor, Joseph S.

Jones, attempted to prevent the gift from being transferred. The black heirs took the case to the county supreme court, where they won a judgment, and each received 94 acres in 1867.[6]

In the years just after the war a few blacks were given title to land by whites who previously had acted as their trustees. For example, in 1866 Philip T. Norwood, a white, gave title of 5 acres in Warren County for $1 to Adam Green, "a free man of color," as Norwood had simply been acting "as trustee for the said Adam Green."[7]

Although only a few county registrars of deeds in other counties in North Carolina denoted the race of those who gained land during these years, even these occasional references to the race of the grantee indicate additional methods and terms upon which blacks gained property.[8] For example, in the town of Edenton, in Chowan County, a number of blacks obtained municipal parcels of land at estate sales. In 1866 Mustaphor McDonald and Job Charlton, both described as men of ":color," made town-lot purchases by virtue of being "the highest and last bidder" at such sales.[9]

If McDonald and Charlton gained their land on the open market in purely financial transactions, other blacks who held traditional ties to the sellers were expected to fulfill largely nonmonetary obligations in order to become landowners. In 1865 Joseph Windsor, of Caswell County, for $1 transferred 50 acres of his land to Esther, who was described as "his former servant woman . . . but now a freed woman of color."[10] Windsor agreed that "for and in consideration of past services rendered and her kind and submissive attention" Esther was entitled to this land. However, he added specific stipulations to the document: Esther had to agree to "wait upon him during his natural life and to cut and make the clothing that he may require to furnish him with good & comfortable shoes as he may need" as well as to do his cooking. Windsor went so far as to specify that he expected her to "furnish me with sugar and coffee as I may need."

Although North Carolina's land deeds between 1865 and 1870 provide a partial glimpse of the process by which blacks gained land during these immediate postwar years, they clearly underrepresent the extent of black landownership five years after the Civil War. Although nearly 4,000 North Carolina black men who headed households owned real estate by 1870, in fact few of them are mentioned in land deeds registered during the late 1860s. For example, five years after the war ended, 293 black men who headed households owned land in Halifax County, but not one is mentioned in a deed registered during this period.[11]

An examination of the status of antebellum African Americans in North Carolina, especially mulattoes, largely explains the landowning situation after the Civil War. While only 8.4 percent of the state's African

Table 1. Real-Estate Ownership by North Carolina African Americans, 1860 and 1870

	1860			1870		
	Percent Owning Real Estate	Average Value	Median Value	Percent Owning Real Estate	Average Value	Median Value
Blacks	21.0	$402	$248	5.2	$329	$200
Mulattoes	25.7	456[a]	293	19.5	369	200
All African Americans	24.3	442[a]	275	6.7	344	200

Source: Manuscript Census of the United States, 1860 and 1870, schedule 1, Alamance through Yancey Counties, North Carolina, Harold B. Lee Library, Brigham Young University, Provo UT.

Note: Only households headed by men are included.

[a]Because in 1860 two mulatto men owned real estate valued so much higher than that of all other men ($26,000 and $15,000), they have been excluded from these averages.

Americans were free in 1860, 71.6 percent of these were mulattoes. Hence, 48.6 percent of the state's mulatto population was free, compared with less than 3 percent of its black population.

Despite the wide difference in their likelihood of being freedmen in 1860, the landowning patterns of blacks and mulattoes who had attained freedom before the war were relatively similar (table 1). Before the war roughly the same percentage of blacks and mulattoes owned land, and the average and median values of the land they possessed were very similar.[12]

In 1860 African-American landowning patterns were not influenced by the region of residence. Although about three-fourths of free African Americans lived in the coastal plain of eastern North Carolina, one-fifth in the piedmont in the central section of the state, and only one-twentieth in the mountains in the west, nearly the same percentage of freedmen in each region owned real estate.[13]

Antebellum black landownership had both an urban and a nonagricultural component. As noted by John Hope Franklin, the foremost scholar on this topic, the free black population in North Carolina, unlike that in most of the other southern states, was overwhelmingly rural and "made their living from the soil."[14] Barely one-tenth of all free blacks lived in towns and cities in 1860. While the rural and agricultural nature of the free black population is not surprising given the fact that the white population was also quite rural and agricultural, it is surprising that those free blacks who resided in urban communities or even held nonagricultural occupations outside the corporate limits of towns and cities formed a significant share of all black real-estate owners. In fact, more than two-fifths of all black landowners made their living outside of agriculture.[15] In those counties with sizable urban communities this group's importance was especially evident. For example, in Craven County slightly more than three-fifths of all black landowners in 1860 were either residents of the town of New Bern or nonagricultural (largely artisans) workers who resided in the surrounding countryside.[16] Collectively the land owned by these nonfarming landowners was valued at 54.3 percent of the value of the land possessed by all free blacks. Although New Bern, with 5,432 inhabitants, cannot be considered a metropolis, even in Granville County, which except for the small village of Oxford was overwhelmingly rural, nonagricultural workers made up the majority of black landowners.[17]

By 1870 the structure of African-American landownership had shifted significantly; it was most evident in the differences between blacks' and mulattoes' landholdings. An examination of the 59,276 households headed by African-American men in North Carolina shows that mulatto men now were nearly four times more likely than black men to own real estate (table 1). This shift in the relative economic standing between the two groups clearly was the result of the sudden emancipation of more than 300,000 blacks compared with only 23,000 mulattoes. And there is reason to suspect that the economic advantage held by mulattoes was even greater than these figures suggest as there was a tendency among census takers to enumerate many mulatto landowners as blacks in 1870.[18]

The origins of the 3,969 African-Americans who owned real estate in 1870 reveal why mulattoes were able to gain an advantage over blacks during the 1860s and perhaps why there were so few land deeds with African-American grantees between 1865 and 1870. However, because the 1870 census takers did not ask blacks and mulattoes whether they had been free before the war or whether they had owned property in 1860, the only way to discover the prewar status of blacks is to compare the 1870 manuscript census with that of 1860. This extremely difficult task is further hindered by five factors: many of the pages of the 1860 manuscript census are illegible; the spelling of names differs markedly between the two censuses; many census takers only noted the initials for the first and middle names of blacks; some blacks changed their names; and most notably, there was extensive migration.[19] This last problem is particularly difficult to overcome since an 1870 black landowner could only be positively identified as having been a freedman in 1860 if he resided in the same county as before the war. The problem is especially acute for those males in 1860 who were too young to head households and therefore had few characteristics, such as the name of a wife or child, to help identify them in both censuses.[20]

The problem of identifying 1870 black landowners as prewar freedmen is best illustrated by reintroducing the case of William S. Williams, the mulatto who bought 2 acres of land in Warren County the day after Christmas in 1865. Williams does not appear in the manuscript census for Warren County in 1860 despite evidence of his having gained his freedom before the war.[21] Perhaps he, like other black landowners in 1870, resided in a different county before the conflict.

Even with the nearly insurmountable problems of trying to link the 1860 and 1870 manuscript censuses, it appears that at least half of the 1870 black landowners may have been antebellum freedmen.[22] Further, these antebellum freedmen owned a substantial share of all of the land owned by blacks in 1870. For example, 38 black men owned a total of $9,750 worth of land in Gates County. Significantly, $7,090 of this land (72.6%) was owned by eighteen men who definitely were free in 1860.[23]

The postwar disparity between mulattoes and blacks had a secondary impact on regional landowning patterns. Although in 1860 there had been very little relationship between where African Americans resided and their likelihood of owning land, in 1870 those residing in the mountains were about twice as likely as those living in the coastal plain and piedmont to be landowners. Significantly, African Americans in the mountains were 50 percent more likely to be mulatto than those in either the coastal plain or the piedmont.[24]

The black landowners in 1870 who can be identified as having been freedmen in 1860 were fairly well off financially before the war. About 50 percent of those men who headed households owned real estate, twice the percentage of all free black male household heads in 1860 and probably only 10–15 percentage points below the level of whites. Most of those men who did not own real estate possessed personal estate that could have been liquidated in order to purchase real estate. Even some of the men who did not head households owned real estate or personal estate. More important, many of these men lived in a home in which the head of the household, usually their father or mother, owned real or personal estate. For example, in 1870 Lewis Pettiford, a 27-year-old mulatto farmer in Granville County, owned land valued at $208. He had been free before the war and had worked as a farm laborer on the land owned by his father, William, valued at $400.[25]

Not only were most of the 1870 landowners who can be documented as having been free in 1860 property owners but those antebellum freedmen who headed households and owned land in 1860 also fared quite well through the war and the first five years of Reconstruction. Despite about a 50 percent decline in land values in North Carolina, the value of land owned by these antebellum black landowners fell by only 5.4 percent.[26] Many, in fact, experienced a rise in property value. For example, Riley Griffen, a mulatto farmer in Martin County, owned land valued at $60 in 1860. By 1870 he owned land valued at $300. Hence, perhaps it is because so much of the land that was owned by blacks in 1870 had already been acquired by 1860 that so few deeds documenting black land acquisition appear after the war.

Even many antebellum free blacks who had not owned land were in a favorable situation for gaining it by 1870. In addition to the 294 landowners who headed households, owned land, and remained during the 1860s in the same county, another 382 of the 1870 black landowners also had been free in 1860. Many of them either gained property on their own during the war or, even more likely, were given it by their parents. For example, in 1860 Dorsey Steward owned no property and resided in Chowan County with his father, Isam, a painter who owned real estate valued at $500. By 1870 the two of them headed separate households, and both were painters. Dorsey now owned land valued at $150, and his father's land was worth $300. If his father gave Dorsey his land, which is likely since his father was approaching his sixtieth birthday, it is unlikely that a deed would have been registered.

One measure of continuity in landownership between 1860 and 1870 was the importance of nonagricultural workers (table 2). Although they constituted only a bit more than one-fourth of the black landowners in 1870, those men who worked outside of agriculture and largely as artisans owned nearly two-fifths of all of the real estate. On average these men, who had such blue-collar skills as carpentry, coopering, blacksmithing, and shoemaking, owned $195 more in real estate than those men who farmed.[27]

The success of nonagricultural black landowners clearly can be linked to emancipation. These men, many of whom had been free before the war but had faced severe restrictions on the exercise of their skills, could employ them in a freer environment during the postwar years, when the number of consumers of their own race was much larger. Further, there were fewer whites to compete against since many white men with similar skills had died in the war.[28] As a result of these new market conditions, those blacks who continued pursuing trades outside of agriculture flourished relative to blacks who had also been free before the war

Table 2. Primary Occupation of Black Landowners, 1870

Occupational Category	Percentage of All Black Landowners	Average Amount Owned
Agriculture[a]	65.5	$297
Laborers[b]	7.1	247
All others[c]	27.4	492

Source: Manuscript Census of the United States, 1870, schedule 1, Alamance through Yancey Counties, North Carolina, Harold B. Lee Library, Brigham Young University, Provo UT.
[a]Includes farmers, farm laborers, farm hands, those who "work on farm," and gardeners.
[b]Includes laborers, day laborers, and common laborers.
[c]Includes professionals, white- and blue-collar workers, and those with no occupation listed.

Table 3. Real-Estate Values of Persistent Landowners by Occupation, 1860 and 1870

Occupational Category	1860		1870	
	Average Value	Median Value	Average Value	Median Value
Agriculture	$364	$200	$389	$200
All others	243	0	527	300

Source: Manuscript Census of the United States, 1860 and 1870, schedule 1, Alamance through Yancey Counties, North Carolina, Harold B. Lee Library, Brigham Young University, Provo UT.
Note: For occupations within categories, see table 2. Only male household heads who remained in the same occupational category between 1860 and 1870 are included here. They need not have owned land in 1860 to be included. There were too few laborers (only 4) to calculate their average and median.

but farmed in both 1860 and 1870. The former group's real estate values more than doubled between 1860 and 1870, while the latter's remained fairly stable (table 3). Therefore, the economic prospects of many antebellum freedmen were enhanced by the general emancipation brought about in 1865.

Although it is fairly easy to document that North Carolina blacks made small gains in land acquisition during the immediate postwar years, their opportunities over the ensuing 45 years are more difficult to determine. Not until after the turn of the century were records kept that provide information on the extent of black ownership of real estate statewide. Therefore, although black ownership can be documented for 1870 using the federal manuscript census and for after 1900 from the records of the state tax commissioner, the pattern during the intervening years can only be discovered by sampling the tax lists of counties that made assessments on a fairly consistent basis.

A sample of five counties—Beaufort, Johnston, and Pasquotank in the coastal plain of eastern North Carolina and Cabarrus and Caswell in the piedmont or central section of the state—reveals clear patterns about the pace of black land acquisition between 1870 and 1915 (tables 4 and 5; see also the appendix). The most striking observation is that even

Table 4. Black Share of Real Estate Statewide and in the
5-County Sample, 1870–1915

| | Value of Real Estate Owned by Blacks | |
	Statewide	in 5-County Sample
1870	1.8%	1.5%
1875	—	2.2
1880	—	2.7
1885	—	3.2
1890	—	3.4
1895	—	4.3
1905	4.5	5.2
1915	6.0	6.1

Source: Manuscript Census of the United States, 1870, schedule 1, Alamance through Yancey Counties, North Carolina, Harold B. Lee Library, Brigham Young University, Provo UT.; Tax Lists of Beaufort, Cabarrus, Caswell, Johnston, and Pasquotank Counties, 1875, 1880, 1885, 1890, 1895; *Report of the North Carolina Corporation Commission as a Board of State Tax Commissioners,* 1906, 1917.

Note: The 1870 percentages are calculated from the manuscript census returns for the 5-county sample and only include households headed by men. For the adjustment of percentages in 1875, 1880, and 1885, see the appendix.

Table 5. Black Share of Real Estate in the 5-County Sample, 1875–1915

| | Black Ownership | | | |
	of Town Lots	of Value of Town Lots	of Acreage	of Value of Acreage
1875	11.4%	3.6%	2.5%	2.0%
1880	16.1	3.6	2.5	2.3
1885	18.3	6.0	3.1	2.9
1890	18.8	6.4	2.8	2.7
1895	21.3	6.8	3.0	3.4
1905	17.9	6.3	4.0	4.5
1915	17.9	7.1	5.2	5.6

Source: Tax Lists of Beaufort, Cabarrus, Caswell, Johnston, and Pasquotank Counties, 1875, 1880, 1885, 1890, 1895; *Report of the North Carolina Corporation Commission as a Board of State Tax Commissioners,* 1906, 1917.

Note: For the adjustment of the percentages in 1875, 1880, and 1885, see the appendix.

as late as 1915 the value of real estate owned by blacks was only 6.0 percent of the value of the total real estate in the state. Despite this low level of landownership, blacks statewide experienced steady, albeit slow, increases, averaging about 1 percent of value of the total real estate in the state every ten years between 1875 and 1915.

Although they were minimal, the gains blacks made statewide need to be considered within the framework of the relative decline in the black share of the population. Blacks increased their share of landownership from 1870 to 1915, but their share of the state population declined from 36.6 percent to 31.6 percent during this period.

Although historical records indicate that their economic progress was slow but steady, at the time blacks may have viewed their pace as just slow. For example, an examination of the early 1880s, which statistically appear to have been better than average years, one year at a time reveals that collectively blacks experienced almost no gains, that some actually suffered losses, and that only a very few made substantive advances. For example, in 1881 there were 65 black landowners in Johnston County. By 1882, 45 of these 65 landowners owned exactly the same amount of real estate as they had owned in the previous year, 12 had experienced an increase, 7 had experienced a decrease (1 actually now owned no land), and 1 apparently had left the county, for his name vanished from the tax list. Of the 12 whose real-estate holdings had increased, the largest gain was experienced by 36-year-old Merritt Holt, whose holdings had risen only from 60 to 88 acres. Only 1 of the other 11 increased his level of ownership by even as much as 20 acres. Of the 6 landowners whose real-estate declined, none lost more than 10 acres. There were 16 new landowners on the 1882 tax list, but an examination of the 1881 list indicates that 15 of them had owned personal estate that year. For example, Bythan McCullers owned 30 acres worth $150 in 1882 after owning no land in 1881; however, although in 1881 McCullers had owned $120 in livestock and other personal property, by 1882 the value of those assets had fallen to only $54. He may have had to sell some of his livestock and personal estate to purchase his land. Some of the new landowners may have inherited rather than purchased their land. For example, Toby, Adam, and Toney Saunders, who ranged in age from 26 to 29 years old, all resided in the Ingrams Tax District of Johnston County in 1882, and all three owned exactly 40 acres of land after owning no land in 1881. It is more than likely, especially since they now owned an equal number of acres, that the three were brothers who had inherited the property from their father during the year.

Altogether, the number of acres owned by blacks in Johnston County increased from 3,694 in 1881 to 4,352 in 1882, an increase of 658 acres. However, half of this increase is accounted for by the holdings of two new landholders who had acquired 316 acres. One of these men had actually sold a town lot that he had owned in 1881 and now owned 155 acres, nearly one-fourth of the acreage increase. In fact, black ownership of town lots actually declined during the year, from 29 to 24 lots. Further, in terms of land value the gain in that year seems especially small: the value of blacks' acreage and town lots increased from $18,520 in 1881 to only $18,732 in 1882.

In Pasquotank County, located about 100 miles northeast of Johnston County on the Albemarle Sound, the pace of land acquisition appears to have been equally slow. Thirty-four of the 52 blacks who owned acreage in Pasquotank in 1880 had title to the identical number of acres in 1881. For those individuals who experienced an increase or decrease in the number of acres they owned, the change was slight. Gains made by the 5 who experienced an increase were very small: 2, 4, 8, 8, and 16 acres. Of the 13 who apparently lost acreage, 4 no longer appeared on the tax roll and had probably moved elsewhere, 5 lost all of their land, and 4 still owned some real estate. The greatest loss matched the greatest gain:

16 acres. There were 7 new landowners, but their landholdings totaled only 150.5 acres. Total acreage owned by blacks increased from 1,417 to only 1,526 acres.

As revealing as 1-year portraits of the pace of land ownership are, even more distinct patterns emerge when the progress of black land acquisition is traced over an entire decade. Fewer than half of the black men who owned rural land in 1880 in the five sample counties continued to do so in 1890. Of the 131 who were fortunate enough to continue owning any land, 46 (35.1%) owned the same number of acres they had owned in 1880. A total of 53 (40.4%) experienced a gain in acreage, and 31 (24.4%) experienced a loss. The median increase was about twice as much as the median loss—12.0 acres compared with 6.7 acres—but both appear quite small. Just 5 of the 53 men who gained acreage accounted for 59.9 percent of the total increase. Finally, age was the most important factor in determining whether a man's holdings rose or declined. Men between 21 and 44 years old were more than twice as likely to gain new acreage as they were to lose it. By contrast, men aged 45 to 49 were more than twice as likely to suffer a loss as they were to enjoy a gain. By 1890 these men, now in their later fifties, probably were passing their land to their mature children.[29]

An important feature of the tax records from this era provides another glimpse of the slow but steady progress of black land acquisition. Because during this period all black men between 21 and 49 years old were supposed to pay a poll, or head, tax, the tax assessors denoted their ages on the tax scrolls. Therefore, it is possible to measure the increase in the number of men in this age group who owned real estate. Between 1875 and 1885 the number of black polls, as they were termed, who owned land doubled (table 6). From 1885 to 1895 more of these men gained land but at a reduced pace.

Moreover, there was a significant difference in the pace at which blacks gained urban and rural land. During the entire period from 1875 to 1895 the number of black urban landowners increased nearly twice as rapidly as did the number of black rural landowners. Overall, during the same era the percentage of black polls who owned either urban or rural land nearly doubled.[30] Thus, although the pace of land acquisition was slow but steady, the trend was definitely one of growth.

Along with a more than doubling in the number of black men who owned rural land from the mid 1870s to the mid 1890s came a decline in the size of holdings, with the median number of acres owned falling by about one-third over the period (tables 6 and 7). This decline in farm size did not, however, signal a reduction in opportunity. Very few of

Table 6. Black Poll Landowners in the 5-County Sample, 1875–95

	Urban Landowners	Rural Landowners	Total Black Landowners
1875	53	214	267
1880	63	295	358
1885	134	399	533
1890	150	447	597
1895	207	490	697

Source: See the 5-county sample in the appendix.

Table 7. Acreage Owned by Black Rural Landowners in the 5-County Sample, 1875, 1885, and 1895

Number of Acres	Percentage Owned by Blacks		
	1875	1885	1895
Fewer than 20	45.3	47.7	56.4
20–99	37.4	44.7	35.4
100–249	14.5	6.6	7.5
250–499	1.9	.7	.6
500 or more	.9	.2	0

Source: See the 5-county sample in the appendix.
   Note: The median number of acres was 22 for 1875, 20 for 1885, and 15 for 1895.

the men who owned fewer than 20 acres had possessed large holdings previously. For example, only 5 of the 26 farmers who owned more than 20 acres in 1880 and lost acreage over the following ten years owned fewer than 20 acres in 1890. In fact, 2 of the 5 were now in their fifties, and like most men of their age, they probably were giving their children some of their land as their own need and ability to work declined. In addition, although their holdings would have been far too small to provide for their families, many of the owners of fewer than 20 acres probably supplemented their income by serving as tenants on other men's

Table 8. Value of Land of Urban and Rural Black Landowners in the
5-County Sample, 1880

Value of Land	Urban Landowners	Rural Landowners
$0–49	4.0%	25.5%
50–99	20.3	24.5
100–249	51.4	31.4
250–499	14.9	11.9
500–999	8.1	5.3
1,000–2,499	1.4	1.3

Source: See the 5-county sample in the appendix.
  Note: The median value was $120 for urban landowners and $100 for rural landowners.
The median age of urban landowners was 32, and that for rural landowners was 37.

land. Hence, their ownership of a few acres symbolized their ability to climb the first rung of the ladder of landownership and economic independence.[31]

One of the most striking aspects of land acquisition by blacks during this period was the variance between opportunity in the countryside and in urban communities. As previously noted, in both 1860 and 1870 blacks residing in urban areas and those with nonagricultural occupations had disproportionate success in gaining land. The ability of blacks with nonagricultural skills to increase their land values during the 1870s was especially remarkable. By 1880 black landownership in the 5-county sample showed similar differences between urban and rural locales (table 8). Although urban black landowners were five years younger than their rural counterparts, a factor that normally would inhibit an individual's chances of owning land, their property values generally were higher. This difference may have resulted from market conditions, which inhibited purchasing very small amounts of town property. Whereas blacks in the countryside could buy and utilize land units as small as a fraction of an acre, urban property could rarely be subdivided into units as small as one-fourth of a lot. A smaller amount of urban property was worthless for either a residence or a place of business. Such a small parcel would only have been valuable for speculation, but few blacks would have had sufficient assets to tie up land for that purpose. Therefore, one-fourth of black rural landowners possessed less than $50 in land, compared with only 4.0 percent of urban black landowners.[32]

Table 9. Value of Real Estate in 1880 of Black Landowners
in the 5-County Sample Who Persisted from 1880 to 1890

Value of Land	Urban Landowners	Rural Landowners
$0–49	11.4%	25.5%
50–99	17.1	25.5
100–249	45.7	31.2
250–499	14.3	12.8
500–999	11.4	4.2
1,000–2,499	0	0.7

Source: See the 5-county sample in the appendix.
　Note: The median value for urban landowners was $200, while that for
rural landowners was $96. The median age for urban landowners was 36,
while that for rural landowners was 38.

Table 10. Decennial Rates of Persistence of Black
Landowners in the 5-County Sample, 1880–90, by Age
and Type of Landownership

Age in 1880	Urban Landowners	Rural Landowners
21–29	36.4%	38.9%
30–39	58.3	48.6
40–49	76.5	49.1
Total	55.6	46.4

Source: See the 5-county sample in the appendix.
　Note: Those landowners whose age in 1880 was not noted on the
tax lists are excluded.

　　The differences in the value of the land they owned in 1880 also was
significantly related to the likelihood of urban and rural black landowners to continue owning land in their communities in 1890 (tables 9
and 10). Not only were black urban landowners more likely than black
rural landowners to remain in their community and continue owning
land, but their land values appreciated at double the rate of rural landowners during the 1880s. However, persisting rural landowners did not

fare poorly. Indeed, the median value of their land rose from $96 to $150. Black urban landowners collectively prospered as well as they did because for about every ten whose land values rose, only one experienced decline.[33]

The collective success of black urban landowners was highlighted and somewhat exaggerated by the remarkable achievement of Warren C. Coleman, of Cabarrus County.[34] Coleman, the illegitimate son of Rufus Clay Barringer, a state legislator and Confederate general, was so light-skinned that a black porter once drove him to a white hotel. When Coleman informed the porter of his error, the porter observed that this was the first time he had encountered a "white colored gentleman." [35] Initially assisted in business by Barringer, Coleman pursued the mercantile trade, starting out with only 2 town lots in Concord worth $600. Within a decade he owned 14.5 town lots with a total worth of $4,950. By 1895, in anticipation of constructing the first black-owned textile mill in the South, Coleman had purchased $13,799 in real estate, including 33.5 town lots and 170 acres.[36]

Perhaps an indication of the relatively equal opportunity black landowners experienced in the countryside and in urban areas, they rarely purchased land in both. Even though the percentage of black polls who owned both forms of land nearly doubled from 1880 to 1890, in 1890 only a handful (2.7%) of landowners could claim possession of both, including only 5.8 percent of the relatively prosperous men who owned land in 1880 and continued to do so in 1890.[37]

Although black rural and urban landowners experienced a nearly identical increase in their real-estate values, by 1895 in the 5-county sample black town residents' share of all town-lot values was twice as large as black farmers' share of all acreage value (table 5). However, whereas the share of town landownership by blacks appears to have peaked in the mid 1890s and subsequently may actually have seen some decline, black rural landowners continued to make steady gains over the next 20 years. Although they never matched their urban counterparts in their share of the ownership of the value of land, by 1915 black rural landowners stood at a closer level than ever before.

A fundamental question is whether black rural landowners lagged behind black townsmen in land acquisition because white farmers discriminated against them more than white urbanites did against black urbanites.[38] Although at first glance this may seem to be the case, it should be recognized that countryside blacks were at a distinct disadvantage in land acquisition because of the social fabric of the rural economy during this era. In a largely agricultural economy with little surplus acreage the average white farmer who sold a part of his land limited his children's options. If a substantial amount of the family estate was sold, some, or all, of the children might have to survive on a smaller share of the land, move elsewhere in order to have enough farmland, or leave the agricultural sector of the economy entirely. Facing the challenge of diminished acreage and a growing population, for many years many white North Carolinians had migrated westward. By the postwar years, however, that solution no longer provided the same opportunities that it had offered previous generations. Now it was necessary to move farther away than ever before, which meant less contact with relatives, and as the recently emancipated blacks were concurrently recognizing, the amount as well as the quality of new acreage in the West did not match the levels of only decades before. Hence, the typical white farmer during this period would have been very reluctant to sell land to anyone, unless, of course, the purchaser could afford to pay a premium price. Few blacks were in such a position.

Land transfers in urban areas, in contrast, may have caused far less social disruption. Although the sale of town lots by white landowners in towns and cities did alter their children's lives, the disruption was far less severe. Property-owning urbanites had always had more career options than had farmers. Urban residents could invest the money they received from the sale of their land in a number of ways which might improve their lives and those of their children within the same or another urban environment. Equally important, urban areas were growing during this period. Although North Carolina continued to be one of the most rural states along the eastern seaboard, its urban population grew from 55,000 in 1880 to 318,474 in 1910. Whereas there had been only 7 communities with more than 5,000 inhabitants in 1880, there were 20 such communities in 1910. Moreover, by 1920, for the first time, two cities, Charlotte and Wilmington, had more than 25,000 residents.

White urbanites were far more likely than white farmers to sell land to blacks, not because white urbanites held less racist attitudes but because they and their families were less personally influenced by the sale. Further, because blacks in urban areas, many of whom had valuable blue-collar skills, were more a part of a cash economy than blacks in the countryside, it would have been easier for them to accumulate the money necessary to make purchases of land.

Black farmers fared better during the period from 1895 to 1915 than they had during the preceding 20 years because of two factors. First, enough blacks gained farm acreage during the 30 years after the war that from 1895 to 1915 more blacks could pass land on to their children than ever before. Second, blacks in the countryside who had purchased or inherited land now had an asset that they might use as collateral to buy other farmland. Even if the number of acres remained constant, the collateral value of their land had increased because of the rising demand for land as the rural population grew. However, most of the better farmland in the countryside was already under cultivation. Because blacks historically had been deprived of landownership as a result of slavery, a disproportionate number may now have been in the market to buy what acreage was for sale. Most white farmers would still have been reluctant to sell their farms, but they were in a position to demand a high price for their land already under cultivation or to sell unimproved land that had never been productive for farming because it was too marshy, hilly, rocky, or forested. The latter type of land would have been far less productive and would have taken considerable labor to improve. Hence, those blacks who did buy farmland at this time paid premium prices even for land of lesser quality. The difference now was that some blacks actually could afford the prices that were asked.

As a result of this combination of factors, from 1905 to 1915 black-owned farm acreage statewide rose by 26.4 percent, compared with only .2 percent for whites.[39] Although more blacks than ever before could afford to buy land, a seller's market existed. Therefore, while the average value per acre of black land rose statewide from $5.40 to $10.03 (an increase of 85.7%), whites only experienced a rise from $5.18 to $8.83 (70.5%).

It is not surprising that the share of the value of acreage owned by blacks exceeded their share of the amount of acreage from 1895 to 1915. Just after the war, when land was cheap because planters facing a future with an unstable labor force were willing to sell their productive acreage, blacks in the countryside had no disposable cash. Now, when many more blacks had assets they could use to buy farmland, the supply of productive but inexpensive land had diminished. They found themselves bidding against one another for what little land was for sale.

Blacks in urban areas faced considerably more favorable circumstances. Because cities continued to grow throughout this period and the number of town lots increased, the urban real-estate market was a much more flexible one for blacks. The greater opportunity in the urban environment compared with that in the rural environment is most evident in the level of homeownership. Whereas 26.2 percent of black household heads residing on farms owned their home in 1890, 32.1 percent did by 1910. Despite this increase, the percentage of rural blacks homeowners was still less than half that of whites, 66.6 percent of whom owned their farm homes in 1910. By contrast, not only did the homeownership of black nonfarm household heads increase dramatically, from 15.1 percent in 1890 to 25.8 percent in 1910, but it was much closer to the

white level of nonfarm homeownership (37.8%) than was that of rural
blacks. Viewed another way, the extent of urban black homeownership
appears even more striking. Despite composing only 16.6 percent of
North Carolina's black population and being both younger and more
likely to be female than the rural black population—factors that generally inhibit homeownership—black urbanites in 1910 composed nearly
half of all black homeowners.[40]

Despite the relatively more favorable circumstances urban blacks
faced in attempting to acquire land, it was black property ownership in
the countryside that most concerned whites during the early twentieth
century. Clarence Hamilton Poe, the editor of the *Progressive Farmer,* the
leading publication about farm life in North Carolina, argued that the
blacks who became landowners during this period actually diminished
the opportunities of non-landowning whites.[41] Under Poe's leadership a
bill was introduced in the state senate in 1915 to bar blacks from acquiring land in a community if a majority of that community's voters or landowners petitioned against land sales to blacks. The leading sectarian
black newspaper in the state, *Star of Zion,* quickly responded by empha-
sizing that the bill clearly violated an individual's civil rights not only because it prevented blacks from buying property but also because it restricted whites from selling property to the highest bidder. "Can a man
be prevented from selling his land for proper consideration to anyone
he chooses? Well, no, but we would so manage to avoid that question
with the old dodge that the Constitution is of little consequence between
friends." The *Star of Zion* pointed out how inconsistent such a proposal
was with whites' traditional encouragement of blacks to "save every dol-
lar [they] can, and to purchase a farm with [their] savings." Further,
referring to the events in Europe, where war had recently broken out,
the newspaper stressed that above all this was a time when all Americans
should "feel secure in their inherent rights."[42]

Although blacks' opposition to the plan probably was of minor consequence politically, many white landowners realized that it would be
more difficult to attract black tenants and to maintain a good market
value for land once blacks' opportunity to purchase land was restricted.
Hence, when only 15 of 32 votes cast in the state senate favored the
amendment, 5 votes short of the three-fifths requirement, the only potential legal restriction North Carolina blacks faced in their quest to
become landowners during the 50 years following emancipation was
defeated.

Although there was no typical rural black landowning family, the history
of Robert and Caroline McGhee, of Granville County, and their descen-

dants demonstrates how black farming families gained and lost real estate during the years 1865 to 1915. While there is strong evidence that
Caroline McGhee and her children were slaves until the end of the Civil
War, the antebellum status of Robert McGhee, Caroline's husband, is less
clear. It is likely that Robert also was a slave, but on a different plantation
in Granville County than the one upon which Caroline and their children were held in bondage.[43]

Even though they believed that they had been married for nearly
25 years in 1865, in the eyes of the law and in point of fact Robert and
Caroline McGhee were treated as chattel before emancipation. It was not
until five years after the Civil War that any document indicated that Robert and Caroline were husband and wife and had a family. In 1870 the
couple, who were then in their forties, owned only $150 in personal es-
tate in Oxford Township, Granville County. Three of their older children
were already married and living on their own. Another decade passed
before a deed was registered specifying that Robert had bought 45 acres
for $365 from Bettie K. Burwell, the widow of Armistead R. Burwell. Un-
til that time Robert probably was a tenant farmer. By 1880, in addition
to the property he had gained from Mrs. Burwell, who appears to have
been a relative of the Littlejohn family of Granville, who had owned
Caroline and some of her children, Robert was farming another 10 acres
of land. He now possessed 20 acres of woodland and 35 acres of tilled
land. In 1879 his farm, which was worth $330, produced 125 bushels of
corn, 15 bushels of oats, 4 bushels of wheat, and 2,000 pounds of tobacco. Except for Robert's oldest son, Frank, who resided nearby on
21 rented acres, all of his sons worked on his farm. Sixteen years later
Robert, now in his seventies, was identified as the owner of 47 acres
in Granville. Despite never experiencing much of an increase in the
amount of real estate they owned, Robert and Caroline held on to their
land until they died, Robert in 1903 and Caroline in 1912.

Frank McGhee actually seems to have gained land of his own before
his parents did. As early as 1876, when he was in his mid thirties, he
owned 7 acres of land worth $35. As in his father's case, the amount of
land Frank owned remained fairly constant. As late as 1915 he possessed
8 acres worth $165. Even though he owned only a small amount of land,
Frank seems to have led a very full life of perhaps more than 100 years.
In addition to both renting and owning land, at one time Frank was the
proprietor of a small store. In 1939, seven years before his death, a Durham city newspaper marked Frank's ninety-sixth birthday by noting that
he was the last Confederate veteran still alive in Granville County. Frank,
who had accompanied his master as a personal servant in Company G of
the Granville Rangers, was cited as remembering the day Stonewall Jack-

3. Frank McGhee, 1939. The son and father of black landowners, he never owned more than a few acres of property.
(8 Oct. 1939, *Durham Morning Herald,* courtesy of *Durham Morning Herald*)

son fell. Frank actually applied for a Confederate pension from North
Carolina in 1928 for his military service; however, there is no record that
he received one.

Although Frank never had very much land of his own, his oldest son,
Joseph, owned 107 acres worth $660 in 1915. This tract of land may have
been part of a larger purchase of 262.8 acres Joseph made in 1909 together with his brother-in-law, Walter Burt. Sometime later Joseph lost
this land either because he could not repay a loan that he had secured
with the land or because of delinquent taxes. Whatever the case, during
the 1920s Joseph and his wife, Cora, decided to move to Montclair, New
Jersey.

David McGhee, Robert and Caroline's second son and fourth child,
appears to have been a tenant farmer until 1885, when he purchased

23⅔ acres from John W. Hays, the trustee of Anna Wimbish. For unknown reasons, by 1895 David and his wife, Rose, had left this farm in Oxford Township and moved to nearby Fishing Creek Township, where David became a sharecropper for Andrew J. Harris, a Vance County lawyer. By 1903, after making scheduled payments to Harris, David became the owner of 100 acres worth $1,492. David died in 1914. Until Rose died, in 1943, she resided with her son Ben, who took over the family farm and managed it until his death, in 1960.

Frederick McGhee, Robert and Caroline's third son, does not appear to have become a landowner until very late in his life as it was not until 1915, when he was in his late fifties, that he was listed as the owner of 12 acres of land worth $165. He may have gained this land as part of his father's will, which was not recorded until 1912, nine years after Robert's death. Robert had specified in his will that after Caroline's death his land should be divided among his nine children. After five of the children conveyed their share of his farm to the other four—and in lieu probably received a cash settlement—the remaining four shares would have been about 12 acres each. Soon after acquiring title to this plot, which Frederick probably already had been farming for some time, he suffered the tragedy of having his home burn down. Rather than remain on the farm and rebuild his home, Frederick moved a few miles east, to the town of Henderson, in Vance County, where he lived until his death, in 1939. Town life was not entirely new for Frederick and his family, as one of his two sons, Alexander, was the owner of a town lot worth $220 at least as early as 1915.

Alexander McGhee, Robert and Caroline's fourth son, was one of the four siblings who gained a share of Robert's estate in 1912. By this time Alexander, like Frederick, was in his fifties. This is the first evidence of his owning land, and he seems to have inherited only 10 acres from his father. His son Ulysses bought this small parcel upon Alexander's death, in 1928.

Robert and Caroline's fifth and youngest son, Thomas, also became one of the owners of Robert's estate in 1912. Thomas's share of 14 acres was appraised at $275 in 1915. Thomas and his wife, Lucy, faced a number of difficulties in their life. Three of their twelve offspring died as children, and Thomas and Lucy had to raise a number of their grandchildren after their mothers, two of Thomas and Lucy's daughters, died in their twenties. Compounding these burdens, when one grandson got into a legal problem and needed money, the farm had to be used as security for a loan. When the loan could not be paid off, the farm was lost. After suffering this financial loss, Thomas and Lucy moved into town. Thomas died in 1947.

In addition to their five sons, Robert and Caroline McGhee had four daughters: Fannie, Amanda, Isabella, and Mollie. Fannie, the eldest daughter, may have been sold away from the family by Caroline's master. By 1866 she apparently had been the wife of Lee Poole for six years. Little is known about Fannie and Lee's life. Lee died in 1895, and by 1900 Fannie was residing in Oxford. She died in 1920.

Amanda, the second daughter, also seems to have been sold away from the family. For many years after the war she lived with her husband, Orchon Faison, in Johnston County, where he was a tenant farmer. Sometime during the 1880s, when word reached the McGhees in Granville that Orchon had died and that Amanda and her children needed help, Robert sent his sons Frank and Tom to bring her and the children to Granville. She moved to Oxford, where she resided until her death, in 1915.

In 1870 Isabella, the fifth child and third daughter, married Isaac Hicks, a tobacco factory worker. By 1880 Isaac had become a farmer and the family was living next door to Robert and Caroline McGhee on 7.5 acres Isaac had purchased in 1874. Isaac died between 1900 and 1910, and Isabella, the mother of ten children, lived until 1934.

Mollie, the youngest child and fourth daughter, married Otis Hicks, a farmer. Otis had been a renter, but by 1910 he had paid off a mortgage on his own farm. In addition, in 1912 Mollie became the only daughter who inherited part of her father's land. Mollie lived on this land until her death, in 1942.

The McGhees' landowning history demonstrates the very slow progress blacks made in acquiring land. Although all five of the McGhee sons at one time in their lives owned land, two of the five only acquired it as a result of inheriting their father's estate, which occurred relatively late in their lives. There was so little land to inherit from Robert that five of his nine children decided to take a cash settlement. Frank purchased land on his own while he was in his thirties, and his small holding remained remarkably stable over the course of his long life. David was the only brother who substantially enlarged his property. He seems to have been the greatest risk taker of the five brothers, as he moved to another part of Granville even after he had purchased a small farm. However, it may be incorrect to give complete credit to David for this decision since in fact he seems to have been afraid to get into a financial situation he felt he might not be able to handle. The McGhee family historian believes it actually may have been due to the encouragement of Rose, his wife, that David bought the much larger farm on time from Andrew Harris.

If only one of Robert and Caroline's five sons experienced true prosperity, many of their grandchildren enhanced their financial status.

Frank's son Joseph did quite well for at least the short term. Even if Joseph's decision to acquire land was linked to his brother-in-law, Walter Burt, considering how few assets his father Frank had acquired, Joseph clearly must have worked hard to gain the money to become a co-investor. Frederick's son Alexander was the first family member to buy a town lot in Granville.

Any measurement of the financial achievement of Robert and Caroline's nine children must take into account the fact that they, like their parents, all started their lives as slaves. When the war ended in 1865 there was no program in place to aid them. Even if there had been a lending institution that could lend them money to buy land, the McGhees had no collateral or credit status. Finally, their one inheritance, their race, was of course an inhibiting economic factor given the attitude of white society. The McGhees' immediate concern was to feed, clothe, and shelter their families. Saving any money and using it to buy their own land often must have seemed just a dream.

Given these factors, it seems all the more remarkable that 50 years after the war ended six of eight male descendants of Robert and Caroline who lived in Granville and appeared on the tax list owned any land. Further, the two who did not own land were only in their twenties at the time. Their opportunities still lay before them. That at least two of Robert and Caroline's four daughters married men who became landowners was equally significant. As for why the McGhees experienced even this degree of success, some credit must be given to Robert and Caroline, who, despite the constraints of slavery, did their best to hold their family together and after emancipation had enough success as tenants to save the money they used to make their land purchase in 1880. They set an example that clearly had an impact on their children.

If the McGhees symbolize the thousands of blacks who acquired small amounts of land between 1865 and 1915, there was also a handful of blacks whose financial advancement was so great that they served as beacons for their entire race of what could be achieved despite adversity. There is no more striking example of a black who emerged from out of nowhere as a prominent farmer than Isaac Forbes, of Craven County, whose accomplishments by the late 1870s even captured the attention of whites.[44] After the fall harvest in 1877 Forbes was described by a white newspaper editor as an "industrious colored man" who recently had come into New Bern "seated in his buggy at the head of a long train, composed of thirty wagon teams, each laden with baled cotton of his own production," which he was having shipped to Baltimore. Although formerly a slave, soon after the war Forbes reportedly purchased a plantation four miles south of New Bern for $5,000 from the prominent Manly family of Craven County. How he obtained the funds was never specified, although it was noted that he not only paid the purchase price in full but also bought a cotton gin and a steam engine. The editor emphasized, "This is an example of industry and perseverance that our colored citizens should take note of and follow with earnestness." And they did. Four years later one of the major black-owned newspapers in the state declared that Forbes, who was "born a slave and started out in life at the end of the war with nothing," was operating a 1,200-acre farm with 15 tenants, who helped him produce between 90 and 100 acres of cotton as well as large quantities of rice, corn, and various other vegetables. Apparently neither the white nor the black editor exaggerated Forbes's accomplishments. In the 1880 agricultural census he was enumerated as the owner of 870 acres worth $5,100. Within the previous year he had paid $2,000 in wages to an all-black labor force, who aided him in producing $3,000 worth of agricultural products.

Among blacks who became substantial landholders in towns, Ashley W. Smith, of Smithfield in Johnston County, stands out.[45] Born a slave in 1852, Smith acquired so large a sum of town property that in 1923, six years before his death, it sold for $31,840. Smith and his mother, Mary, had been slaves on the Bryant Smith plantation in Johnston County. By working for an in-law of his former master just after the war, Smith earned $140, which formed the "nucleus of the considerable fortune" he eventually accumulated. In 1875, while he was in his early twenties, he purchased his first piece of town property in Smithfield. Within ten years he had increased his holdings to 36 acres worth $250 and three town lots worth $3,000. By 1918, with the earnings he had made as a merchant and his wife Lina had made as a dressmaker, Smith had bought land on at least 15 occasions, from both white and black landowners. The center of his holdings was a 2-story building in downtown Smithfield that housed a number of black-operated firms and functioned as the social center for the black community. In addition to his real-estate holdings and business endeavors, Smith served on the Smithfield board of town commissioners during the 1890s.

If Ashley Smith exemplified what a black landowner could achieve in a small town, Isaac Smith, of New Bern in Craven County, demonstrated the success that could be attained in a city.[46] Smith may have been the wealthiest black in North Carolina at the time of his death, in 1915. Although Smith's early years are obscure, he does not appear to have been born into a landholding antebellum black family. Apparently, he did gain some education from a white family, which allowed him later to attend the black Episcopal institution in Raleigh, St. Augustine's College. By the early 1870s he was recorded as buying and selling property in Craven County at the same time that he was teaching school. After he left teaching, he earned a living lending money and selling insurance. Soon he began to focus on real-estate investments in New Bern. He owned so many stores and houses in one part of the city that this section was referred to as "Smithtown." After making his mark in realty, he became involved in politics as an active member of the Republican Party. An early endorser of William McKinley for president, he was considered one of the state's largest donors to the party. In 1898 he was elected to the state house from Craven County. His two years of service proved to be quite stormy as he was expelled from the party caucus for allying himself too closely with the Democrats in the legislature. With the passage of legislation in 1900 that would lead to the disfranchisement of most blacks in North Carolina, Smith left politics and renewed his efforts in real estate. When he died in 1915 his estate was appraised at $110,000, of which $100,000 was in real estate. In his will he left considerable sums to black educational, religious, and fraternal institutions.

Any examination of the pace of black land acquisition during the 50 years following the Civil War must recognize that blacks did not begin their quest to gain real estate in 1865. Before the war, the small population of freedmen, largely mulattoes, were already laying the foundation that would exist following the general emancipation. That foundation was particularly strong for those blacks who labored outside of agriculture and resided in urban communities. Over the next 30 years this group made remarkable gains in property ownership as they found the urban real-estate market to be both expansive and flexible. If blacks in agriculture initially lagged behind their urban neighbors, they also established a pace of growth that would begin to accelerate during the 1890s, when they nearly doubled the amount and value of acreage they owned from 1890 to 1915. Every ten years from 1865 to 1915 black landowners as a whole would gain ownership of about 1 percent of the value of real estate in North Carolina, even though the black percentage of the state population would actually decline. Though adverse social, economic, and political circumstances prevented most blacks from becoming landowners by 1915, a significant number of blacks overcame these challenges to possess land in their own name.

2

The Black Business Community

IN 1829 Alfred Hargrave was born a slave in Davidson County.[1] Except for the names of his parents, John and Betty, nothing else is known about Hargrave's early years. Sometime during the 1850s Hargrave, who had been trained as a blacksmith, was hired out by his master to work for the Atlantic Coast Line Railroad Company for $1,200 a year in Wilmington. In 1859 Hargrave received permission from the president of the railroad company, Colonel P. K. Dickerson, to spend his lunch time earning money shoeing horses. Nicey, Hargrave's wife, would bring him his lunch and help him blow the bellows while he ate and worked.

When the war ended, and with the knowledge he had gained from this partial self-employment, Hargrave set up his own blacksmith firm in Wilmington, on the north side of Market Street, between 7th and 8th Streets. He later moved his shop to the southeast corner of 7th and Princess Streets. As evidence of his success, by 1870 Hargrave owned $2,900 in real estate in Wilmington, and he continued to prosper in his trade over the next three decades.

When he died in 1898, Hargrave's firm, which had already been in business for nearly forty years, was continued by his sons, John and Moses, and his grandson, Garnett. They maintained the company until 1938, when blacksmithing and horseshoeing no longer were lucrative. Conscious of the circumstances surrounding the company's beginnings and their ancestor's achievement, Hargrave's descendants proudly ad-

4. Alfred Hargrave. (Courtesy of Cape Fear
Museum, Wilmington NC, IA 883, Sadgwar
Collection)

vertised on the wall outside of their shop that the enterprise had been in
continuous operation since 1859.

Alfred Hargrave's remarkable story of long-term success raises a number of important questions about North Carolina blacks who operated
businesses in the postwar years.[2] Did blacks who were, like Hargrave,
businessmen during the fifty years after the war have antebellum experience in their trade? Did they locate primarily in large cities such as
Wilmington, which had substantial black populations? Did they find as
much success as Hargrave?

The nature of the black business community during the immediate postwar years is revealed in the credit ratings from 1865 to 1880.[3] When
supplemented by other sources, these credit ratings describe numerous
characteristics of black entrepreneurs and their businesses: their age,
type of firm, years in business, the nature of their clientele, and their

5. Hargrave & Son, ca. 1914. According to the descendants of Alfred Hargrave, he started the family's blacksmith firm in 1859 (note year in horseshoe at *upper left*), while he was still a slave. (Courtesy of Cape Fear Museum, Wilmington NC, IA 1691, Sadgwar Collection)

property holdings. One can also discover whether these men were freedmen or slaves before the Civil War, whether they owned slaves, the role of family ties in their enterprises, the nature of their partnerships, personal and business connections with whites, the value of their firms, and most important, an evaluation of their personal character as well as of their business qualifications.

Although one might expect these personal evaluations of black businessmen to be racist in tone since they were written by white Southerners, many demonstrate high respect for the character of black businessmen. For example, J. B. Alford, a black general storekeeper in the village of Smithfield, in Johnston County, who was evaluated on a continual basis from June 1866 to May 1878, was described in December 1869 as "a very respectful and energetic man of color doing considerable business and I think very reliable." By May 1877 the value of his real and personal estate was estimated at $3,450. Likewise, when Alfred Hargrave, the Wilmington blacksmith who had learned his trade under slavery, was rated in June 1879, he was termed "a worthy colored man." Equally important, credit raters could be quite frank in their evaluations. Richard Jones, a black general storekeeper in the community of Halifax Court House in Halifax County, in June 1873 was referred to as a "purchaser of stolen goods, a great scamp."[4]

The credit-rated black business firms in North Carolina between 1865 and 1880 were not clustered in any one location but were scattered throughout 30 different counties and had 46 different post office designations (table 11). The vast majority of them were found in the eastern part of the state, where most of the black population resided; slightly more than one-tenth of the black firms were located west of Raleigh.[5]

There was a clear relationship between the percentage of a county's population that was black and the number of black firms it supported (table 11). The counties in which two-thirds or more of the residents were black—Warren, Halifax, and Edgecombe—were ranked first, second, and fourth in the number of black firms they supported. Only Wake County, which contained the city of Raleigh, the second largest community in the state, had more than ten black firms.

In those counties with one or more black credit-rated firms the black population approached nearly half of the total population, compared with their statewide average of slightly more than one-third. By comparison, in those counties without black credit-rated firms blacks composed only about one-fourth of the total population. Even more indicative of the relation was the percentage of the population that was black in the villages, towns, and cities where black firms generally were located: slightly more than 50 percent.[6]

The exact clientele of these black firms is difficult to determine because business ledgers, which usually note the names of customers and are quite numerous for white entrepreneurs, have not survived for black establishments.[7] Nevertheless, since black entrepreneurs located their firms in counties and communities with the highest concentration of blacks in the state, one can speculate that most of their customers were black. However, it would be incorrect to assume that all of the customers of such firms were black.

Advertising provides one indication that whites may have frequented black firms. State and local business directories from this era reveal that black businessmen never denoted their race in advertisements even though this might have increased the size of their black clientele. Of course, for most black and white customers this was probably an insignificant issue as they probably knew all of the black businessmen in their

Table 11. Location of Black Firms in R. G. Dun & Co. Credit Ledgers, 1865–79

County:	Blacks as % of Total Population, 1870	Number of Black Firms	Post Office of Firms	Number of Firms at Post Office	Total Population at Post Office, 1870	Blacks as % of Total Population at Post Office, 1870
Warren	70.3	11	Warrenton	10	941	56.7
			Ridgeway	1	—	—
Halifax	66.6	10	Halifax Court House	3	429	69.9
			Weldon	3	208	64.4
			Enfield	3	—	—
			None listed	1	—	—
Edgecombe	65.8	12	Tarboro	8	1,340	48.7
			Rocky Mount	1	357	46.8
			Battleboro	1	—	—
			Keyesville	1	—	—
			Wilson	1	—	—
Craven	59.0	8	New Bern	8	5,849	65.9
New Hanover	57.9	8	Wilmington	8	13,446	58.9
Northampton	57.7	7	Jackson	2	181	46.4
			Garysburg	1	—	—
			Pleasant Hill	2	—	—
			Rich Square	2	—	—
Bertie	57.4	1	Windsor	1	427	53.4
Granville	53.8	8	Henderson	3	545	55.2
			Oxford	3	916	49.4
			Kittrell	1	—	—
			Townsville	1	—	—
Hertford	53.4	1	Winton	1	—	—
Franklin	53.1	5	Franklinton	3	305	34.4
			Louisbourg	2	750	53.3
Lenoir	53.0	3	Kinston	3	1,103	53.3
Chowan	52.2	6	Edenton	6	1,243	—
Greene	52.0	1	Hookerton	1	163	46.6
Pitt	48.7	5	Greenville	5	601	49.6
Pasquotank	48.6	1	Elizabeth City	1	930	45.3

continues

Table 11. *Continued*

County:	Blacks as % of Total Population, 1870	Number of Black Firms	Post Office of Firms	Number of Firms at Post Office	Total Population at Post Office, 1870	Blacks as % of Total Population at Post Office, 1870
Martin	47.5	4	Jamesville	2	150	32.7
			Hamilton	1	200	60.0
			Roanoke	1	—	—
Wake	45.4	11	Raleigh	11	7,790	52.6
Robeson	45.3	1	Lumberton	1	615	46.2
Wayne	44.9	1	Goldsboro	1	1,134	39.4
Cumberland	44.1	4	Fayetteville	4	4,660	49.7
Mecklenburg	44.1	2	Charlotte	2	4,473	42.0
Washington	42.6	4	Plymouth	4	1,389	58.1
Orange	36.7	1	Chapel Hill	1	—	—
Beaufort	35.6	1	Washington	1	2,094	52.9
Chatham	34.6	1	Pittsboro	1	—	—
Rowan	31.6	2	Salisbury	2	168	60.1
Johnston	30.7	2	Smithfield	2	415	48.7
Guilford	28.0	2	High Point	2	—	—
Burke	23.7	2	Morganton	2	554	40.4
Stokes	23.3	1	Danbury	1	—	—
Average	47.7	126		126		54.7
State average	36.6					

Sources: North Carolina vols. 1–25, R. G. Dun & Co. Collection, Baker Library, Harvard University Graduate School of Business Administration, Boston; U.S. Census Office, *The Statistics of the Population of the United States in June 1, 1870* (Washington DC: GPO, 1873), 52–54, 220–26.

Note: The 1870 published censuses do not enumerate the total populations or black populations of communities for which no data are provided.

communities, which generally contained only a few hundred residents. However, even in the state's largest communities, which had populations in the low thousands and where the race of the firms' owners would have been less well known, there seems to have been no effort by black businessmen to stress their race.[8]

JAMES LOWREY,

MANUFACTURER OF

CARRIAGES, BUGGIES, WAGONS, CARTS AND DRAYS,

4th Cor. Campbell, Wilmington, N. C.

☞ Painting and Trimming neatly executed.

☞ Old Buggies and other vehicles repaired and renovated in the most thorough manner.

☞ New Work kept for sale, at low prices.

☞ Being an old citizen of Wilmington, and having had thirty years experience in my business, I respectfully ask the public to give me a trial.

---

6. James Lowrey advertisement, 1877. Lowrey emphasized his many years in business and his long residence but did not note his race. (From William Henry Beveridge, comp., *Beveridge and Co.'s North Carolina State Directory, 1877–78* [Raleigh: News Publishing Company, n.d.], 442)

Some black businessmen may even have tried to gain white customers by obscuring their race. For example, James A. Lowrey, a black carriage maker in Wilmington, in an advertisement appearing in a statewide business directory during the late 1870s not only emphasized that he sold his "new work" "at low prices" but added that his "being an old citizen of Wilmington, and having thirty years experience" in his business merited that "the public" give him "a trial."[9] A potential customer who did not know Lowrey's race, which was a possibility in the state's largest city, might assume from such an advertisement that this long-established firm was conducted by a white craftsman. In some communities blacks were the only businessmen conducting certain trades, so whites had no choice but to patronize them. Therefore, although it appears, given the racial composition of the communities having black firms, that most of the customers of black businessmen were black, whites may have composed a significant share of their customers.

If the nature of the clientele of credit-rated black firms remains somewhat obscure, the types of black businesses and their structure is much clearer. Mercantile firms, which included grocery, provision, and general merchandise dealers, although not a majority, were the most common type of black enterprises (table 12). Four-fifths of the black firms were proprietorships. Interestingly, businesses operated by relatives were the exception; only two were described in the credit ledgers of this pe-

Table 12. Type and Structure of Credit-Rated Black Firms, 1865–79

Type of Firm	Number	Percentage of Total Firms	Proprietorships as Percentage of Total Firms
Mercantile	53	42.1	69.8
Skilled trades	28	22.2	92.6
Liquor	12	9.5	91.2
Liquor-mercantile	9	7.1	88.9
Not specified	7	5.5	71.4
Confection and confection-liquor	6	4.8	100.0
Diversified	6	4.8	100.0
Other	3	2.4	100.0
Service	2	1.6	100.0
Total	126	100.0	82.5

Source: North Carolina vols. 1–25, R. G. Dun & Co. Collection, Baker Library, Harvard University Graduate School of Business Adminstration, Boston.

riod: J. W. Lee & Bro., of Edenton, in Chowan County, and S. A. Perry & Sons, of Tarboro, in Edgecombe County.[10] Although the majority of all types of firms were single proprietors, the greater capital necessary to purchase or rent a building and stock a diverse supply of goods caused nearly one-third of mercantile establishments to be structured as partnerships or companies.

Only one firm, Andrew Boone & Co., a general store in the village of Jackson, in Northampton County, seems to have included a large number of partners. Andrew Boone, an illiterate 27-year-old black, began operating a general store in July 1874. For five years he barely kept his business intact, and the credit rater continually advised that Boone be shipped goods on credit only with caution. By March 1879, probably in an attempt to put his business on a firmer financial basis, Boone took on what were described as "about 20 Negroes who place in the business about $10 each." Since the last evaluation of the company's credit was made in December 1879, it is impossible to determine whether the assets of the new black stockholders enhanced the firm. In 1880 Boone was still enumerated as a merchant in the census.[11]

Partnerships between black and white businessmen were just as uncommon as black-owned companies with numerous black partners or shareholders. Only one black credit-rated firm—Henry Harper, James Ransom & Co., carriage makers in Warrenton in Warren County—was composed of both white and black partners. After the establishment's formation in February 1867, the credit rater noted that Harper, "a white man," was conducting the firm with "two colored" partners and added that "all three were hardworking, prudent, & energetic men." Although it is impossible to explain why Harper formed a business with two blacks—one of whose names was never mentioned and who left the firm in 1869—two factors may have led the other black, James Ransom, to become Harper's partner. First, James Ransom had been a 17-year-old free black working as a coachmaker before the Civil War, and he probably was one of the most qualified tradesmen in this field in Warrenton when he and Harper became partners. Second, Ransom was described in a community history as a "Negro leader who supported the Conservative party" during Reconstruction, a particularly unusual stance for a black in Warren County.[12] Perhaps his political position made him socially acceptable as a partner for Harper. Ransom was so well respected in the community that he was elected to the county commission, the chief local governing board. Harper and Ransom stayed in business together for ten years.

The most unifying characteristic of the credit-rated entrepreneurs was their skin color; more than half of them were mulattoes (tables 13 and 14).[13] Mulattoes were overrepresented among the ranks of African-American entrepreneurs after the war for the same reason that they were overrepresented among African-American landowners, namely, because compared with most blacks a disproportionate number of mulattoes were free before the war and thus had a significant headstart.

All of the African Americans who were businessmen during the fifteen years following the war and had been free in 1860 were mulattoes, and most of them were involved in the trade they had conducted before the war.[14] This pattern has already been described in the case of James Ransom, the mulatto carriage maker in Warrenton. It was also true for John Mayzek, a mulatto resident of Morganton, in Burke County, whom a credit ledger described in May 1860 as a free black "barber . . . [who] keeps a liquor shop & candies." He owned property valued at $400. After the war Mayzek continued his barber trade in Morganton. Indicative of his excellent business skills, and representative of all the mulattoes who ran both antebellum and postbellum businesses, Mayzek increased the value of his estate during the war and immediate postwar years and by 1870 possessed $700 in property. Similarly, Matthew Leary, a free mulatto saddler in Fayetteville, in Cumberland County, in 1860 was conducting the business he had established in the same location in 1848.

Table 13. Property Values of Credit-Rated African-American Businessmen, 1870

Dollars	Real Estate		Total Estate	
	Mulattoes (N = 32)	Blacks (N = 22)	Mulattoes (N = 32)	Blacks (N = 22)
0	5.6%	27.3%	0%	13.6%
1–99	0	9.1	0	4.5
100–249	3.1	9.1	12.5	4.5
250–499	25.0	22.7	6.2	18.2
500–999	25.0	13.6	34.4	27.3
1,000–2,499	21.8	13.6	28.1	22.7
2,500+	9.4	4.5	18.8	9.1
Median value	$500	$250–300	$700–950	$500–550

Source: Manuscript Census of the United States, 1860 and 1870, schedule 1, Alamance through Yancey Counties, North Carolina, Harold B. Lee Library, Brigham Young University, Provo UT.

Note: If a businessman was listed as mulatto either in 1860 or 1870 census, he is designated as mulatto in this table.

Table 14. Type of Firm by Race of Credit-Rated African-American Businessmen, 1865–79

Type of Firm	Mulattoes	Blacks
Mercantile	32.4%	44.8%
Diversified [a]	16.2	0
Skilled trades	29.7	31.0
Liquor-mercantile	10.8	10.3
Liquor	5.4	3.4
Confection and confection-liquor	2.7	6.9
Service	0	3.4
Other	2.7	0

Source: Manuscript Census of the United States, 1860, 1870, and 1880, schedule 1, Alamance through Yancey Counties, North Carolina, Harold B. Lee Library, Brigham Young University, Provo UT.

[a] All but one diversified firm were partly mercantile.

From September 1865 through December 1879, when the manuscript credit ratings ended, Leary, who owned no property in 1860 but possessed $5,000 in real estate and $1,000 in personal estate in 1870, continued to run his saddlery firm.[15]

Having been emancipated at least a half-decade longer than most of their black neighbors, mulattoes were able to dominate the African-American business community for at least the first five years after the war. By 1870 four-fifths of the African Americans who had run businesses since 1865 were mulattoes. Although after 1870 the number of mulattoes and blacks who joined the entrepreneurial ranks was about even, mulattoes were still disproportionately represented, constituting about half of the new businessmen. Further, although they generally ran the same types of firm as blacks, because of the long-term impact of their antebellum freedom, the value of mulatto businessmen's property continued to be higher, and they were slightly more likely to be literate, factors that permitted them a wider variety of business options (tables 13 and 14).[16]

Although mulattoes generally were wealthier than blacks, for slightly more than four-fifths of both groups proprietorships were the most common form of business structure. However, blacks were more than twice as likely as mulattoes to form 2-member partnerships.[17] It may have been more necessary for blacks to take on partners simply because they generally possessed less capital. Further evidence of this disparity is revealed in an examination of all North Carolina blacks and mulattoes involved in the mercantile trade. The median total estate of black merchants and grocers ranged between $500 and $550, compared with $1,100 for mulattoes. Equally significant, both of the 2-member partnerships—which did engage in the mercantile trade—were composed of two blacks. There is no evidence of a mulatto ever forming a partnership with a black, although there is the case of James Ransom, the mulatto carriage maker who formed a partnerships with a white.

The factors that differentiated mulatto and black businessmen in North Carolina may have had an impact on the degree of success African-American businessmen experienced. Those who started their businesses immediately after the war—largely mulattoes emancipated in the antebellum period—were much more likely to survive in business for a long period of time than those who began in the 1870s, who increasingly were likely to be black (table 15). There are a number of interrelated reasons for this finding. Businessmen running firms just after the war's conclusion were much more likely than those who started businesses in the 1870s to have been free before the war; hence they were far more experienced in business than those who were freed during the Civil War.

Table 15. Success Rates of Credit-Rated Black Firms, 1865–80

Period Created	Number of Years Firms Lasted					Total Number
	1 or More	2 or More	3 or More	4 or More	5 or More	
1865–67	100.0%	100.0%	85.7%	85.7%	85.7%	7
1868–72	87.2	66.7	59.0	53.8	46.7	39
1873–74	73.9	60.9	47.8	30.4	26.1	23
1875–78 [a]	97.0	85.7	50.0	44.4		34
1879–80 [b]						23
Total						126

Source: North Carolina vols. 1–25, R. G. Dun & Co. Collection, Baker Library, Harvard University Graduate School of Business Administration, Boston.

[a]No firm created during this period could have lasted five years since the credit ledgers ceased before the end of 1880. The percentage of firms that lasted between two and four years is based only on those that possibly could have stayed in business that long given the conclusion of the records.

[b]Rates cannot be determined for these years because the credit ledgers ceased before the end of 1880.

Many of them had survived and prospered in business through the war, an accomplishment that probably would have distinguished many even from their white antebellum entrepreneurial peers. Moreover, antebellum businessmen survived even though the size of their black clientele was limited until the war's conclusion. When the war ended they were in an ideal position to take advantage of a vastly enlarged market of African-American consumers. A few such entrepreneurs apparently used this opportunity to corner the black economy in their villages, towns, and cities.

For a businessman who was both black and a former slave, the role of his antebellum experience in his respective fields also could be critical. The abovementioned Alfred Hargrave, who was black, had the advantage under slavery of learning the blacksmithing trade and earning money. He clearly must have been particularly skilled in order for his master to be able to hire him out for $1,200 a year. The experience he gained and the reputation he developed while applying his trade as a slave in Wilmington clearly placed him in a favorable position when the war ended.

The long-term success of these early entrants into the black business community was enhanced by their having already carved out a share of the market in their communities before the national business panic began in 1873. By contrast, those blacks and mulattoes who established firms in 1873 and 1874 entered the business arena at the worst possible time. Not only did they have to compete against individuals who already had been in business for a number of years but they had to do so at a time when it was terribly difficult to gain credit, a necessity for the success of almost any business. Once the depression of the mid 1870s began to abate, the rate of success of new entrants began to approach, although it never quite matched, that of the earlier entrants (table 15).

A final factor inhibiting the success of new entrants into the black business community during the depression was their relative youth. Whereas the early entrants had a median age of 39 years, the new entrants from 1873 through 1875 had a median age of only 31 years.[18] This may also explain why their property values were lower than those of their predecessors and perhaps those of the new businessmen who followed them.

Given their diverse economic advantages over later entrants, it is not surprising that those who were early participants in the postwar business environment established an exceptional success rate. In fact, their rate of success compared quite favorably with, and in some cases even exceeded, that of the southern white merchants of this era, a group that Roger Ransom and Richard Sutch have identified as being remarkably successful during the 1870s (table 16). Perhaps these early businessmen flourished for the same reason as the one Ransom and Sutch proposed for the success of white merchants, namely, because they had created a territorial monopoly.[19] Whether they intended to or not, because of their knowledge of the black consumer in North Carolina—a group of limited size and resources—those first black businessmen simply dominated their communities' markets. Further, since early entrants into the black business community had to deal routinely with adverse economic conditions, they were better prepared to cope with the depression of the 1870s than were the whites, who, though they generally held greater assets and definitely served a larger and more diverse clientele, were less familiar with the business skills necessary to succeed during hard times.

Diversification was an additional advantage that permitted some of these early black businessmen to succeed. Six black firms can be classified as diversified based on the wide range of enterprises they encompassed in their communities (table 12). The career of Allen Evans, a mulatto businessman in Wilmington, in New Hanover County, illustrates the importance of diversification. Although it is not known whether

Table 16. Success of Credit-Rated Southern White and North Carolina Black Firms, 1870–75 and 1870–80

Type of Firms Active in 1870	Number	Firms Still Active in			
		1875		1880	
		%	No.	%	No.
White mercantile firms (Ransom and Sutch southern white mercantile sample)	38	71.0	27	55.3	21
All types of North Carolina black firms	15	73.3	11	46.7	7
North Carolina black mercantile firms	9	77.8	7	55.6	5

Sources: North Carolina vols. 1–25, R. G. Dun & Co. Collection, Baker Library, Harvard University Graduate School of Business Administration, Boston; Roger Ransom and Richard Sutch, *One Kind of Freedom: The Economic Consequences of Emancipation* (Cambridge: Cambridge University Press, 1977), 142–44.

Evans was free before the war, by January 1866 he had started a combination barbershop and grocery that was worth between $1,000 and $2,000. By 1870 Evans owned $3,200 in property. During the 1870s he also included the liquor trade among his endeavors. His dominance of a number of sectors of the local economy stifled all of his competitors. Thomas Rivera, a mulatto who tried to compete with Evans by opening a Wilmington grocery in 1868, failed within a year and a half. H. Brook, who in June 1874 opened a Wilmington bar that might have cut into Evans's market, failed within six months.[20] All six of the diversified firms were run by mulattoes. Four of the six survived at least to 1880. Even the two that closed earlier were not unsuccessful: one dissolved after the firm's owner died, and the owner of the other company apparently retired in his late eighties.

Their inability to relocate at another site particularly must have frustrated the black businessmen who failed to capture a share of a community's black patrons. None of the five black businessmen who failed and moved to another community was later documented as conducting a business at his new location. For example, John Batchelor tried to run a grocery in Warrenton beginning in 1868. Although Warrenton had a substantial black population and the surrounding countryside offered one of the highest proportions of blacks of any section of the state, Batchelor's task was not easy because the town's black business community was dominated by two mulattoes, John Plummer and William S. Williams, who conducted mercantile firms as well as dabbling in the confection, liquor, transport, butchering, and livery businesses. Although he was characterized as a man of "good habits & character" and "good intentions," by December 1872 Batchelor had had little success, was "totally insolvent," and decided to relocate 50 miles to the south, in Raleigh. However, he was never recorded as establishing a business in Raleigh, nor does he subsequently appear in the ledger for any other North Carolina county. It would be unjust to blame John Plummer, William S. Williams, or any other successful black businessman for John Batchelor's failure. Although both Plummer and Williams experienced unusual success, they probably did not intend to cause other blacks to fail.[21]

Beyond the immediate postwar years, between 1880 and 1905 the black business community experienced two trends: the number of black credit-rated firms increased nearly fourfold; and the number of communities with at least one such firm increased nearly threefold.[22] Although the growth in the number of black firms was remarkable, it was also quite inconsistent (table 17). During the years 1880–85 the number of firms nearly doubled; however, the downturn in North Carolina's economy during the late 1880s and the national depression of the mid 1890s prevented another doubling from occurring until 1905.

The geographic expansion of black firms was equally inconsistent. The doubling in the number of black businesses during the first half of the 1880s resulted from two factors. First, in some locations the size of the black business community increased. For example, although Edenton's population remained fairly stable from 1880 to 1885, the number of black firms within the village grew from three to five during these years. Likewise, in the village of Jamesville the number of black credited-rated firms increased from two to five during the first half of the 1880s. Second, other black entrepreneurs created new markets in communities that had never had black establishments. For example, during the early 1880s Green Oliver opened a general store and H. H. Curtis opened a confectionery in the village of Milton, in Caswell County, a community that had never had a black firm.

This rapid increase in the number of black firms during the 1880s further diminished the success individual black establishments experienced. During the period 1870–1910, firms experienced their lowest decennial rate of persistence in the 1880s (table 18). In part, the influx of new black competitors in their communities may have caused some existing blacks firms to fail. In Edenton John R. Page, who had sold fish

Table 17. Communities with Black Firms, 1880–1905

Year	Number of Firms	Number of Communities with at Least 1 Firm
1880	84	39
1885	165	68
1890	200	73
1900	273	109
1905	320	116

Source: *Mercantile Agency Reference Book*, 1880, 1885, 1890, 1900, 1905, Library of Congress, Washington DC. The Library of Congress does not have a copy of the 1895 *Mercantile Agency Reference Book*.

Note: The credit ratings list the name of the firm's nearest post office and not necessarily the exact community in which the firm was located.

Table 18. Decennial Rates of Persistence of Black Firms by Region, 1870–1910

Years	Coastal Plain	Piedmont	Mountain	Total
1870–80	46.7%	—	—	46.7%
1880–90	22.2	8.3%	—	20.2
1890–1900	24.2	29.7	0%	25.0
1900–1910	35.1	17.9	25.0	30.0

Source: *Mercantile Agency Reference Book,* 1870, 1880, 1890, 1900, 1910, Library of Congress, Washington DC.

since the late 1870s, had ceased doing so by 1885. Exactly why Page's business closed is unclear. Perhaps Jones & Charlton, one of the new competing black-run general stores, drove him out of business by supplying a more complete line of goods. By contrast, J. W. Draper, who had been running a stove store in Edenton for as long as Page had sold fish and who faced no new competition, remained in business until at least 1905.

A year-by-year analysis of ratings also reveals that far more firms existed during the 1880s than is suggested by an examination of the 84 establishments existing in 1880 and the 200 existing in 1890. In fact, between 1880 and 1890 the total number of firms was more than 500. In other words, every month during the decade 3.5 new firms opened their doors for the first time and 3.1 existing firms closed their doors for the last time.[23]

Undercapitalization largely explains why after 1880 the black business community failed to enjoy the high rates of success it had experienced immediately after the Civil War. In 1880 black establishments were only one-tenth as likely as white firms to have a pecuniary strength (the net worth of the proprietor) of at least $2,000. Furthermore, the average pecuniary strength of black firms continued to slide over the next two decades. Between 1880 and 1900 the share of all black firms with a pecuniary strength of at least $2,000 decreased by half. Even more striking was the limited share of all black firms having a pecuniary strength of even $1,000: 19.0 percent in 1880, 12.0 percent in 1890, and only 5.1 percent by 1900.[24]

Besides undercapitalization, the constant turnover of firms can be linked directly to the inability of most communities to sustain more than a small handful of black firms. For example, the village of Jamesville began and ended the 1880s with only one mercantile firm despite the presence of four such firms during the decade.

The fortunes of black businessmen who created new markets was also mixed. James Cross opened a combination grocery and liquor store in the village of Hamilton, in Martin County, during the early 1880s. By 1890 he had failed, and no black firm ever again was credit-rated in that village, an indication that no black enterprises located there. By contrast, the previously noted Green Oliver, who initiated a general store in Milton during the same period, was able to survive in business for more than two decades. Oliver's success is especially remarkable because soon after he opened the first black-owned firm in Milton he was joined by a black competitor, G. F. Bowers, who remained in business for at least ten years. Clearly, James Cross miscalculated his chances for success as a black en-

Table 19. Credit-Rated Black Firms by Region, 1870–1905

	Coastal Plain		Piedmont		Mountain		
	No.	% of Total	No.	% of Total	No.	% of Total	Total
1870	15	100.0%	0	0.0%	0	0.0%	15
1875	50	89.3	6	10.7	0	0.0	56
1880	72	85.7	12	14.3	0	0.0	84
1885	136	82.4	27	16.4	2	1.2	165
1890	161	80.5	37	18.5	2	1.0	200
1900	191	70.0	78	28.6	4	1.5	273
1905	243	75.9	63	19.7	14	4.4	320

Source: Mercantile Agency Reference Book, 1870, 1875, 1880, 1885, 1890, 1900, 1905, Library of Congress, Washington DC.

trepreneur in Hamilton, but Green Oliver identified a good market in Milton.

The success Green Oliver encountered in Milton is indicative of another important component of the development of black firms in North Carolina after 1880. Milton, in Caswell County, was within the piedmont section of central North Carolina. Whereas during the first fifteen years after the war black firms were concentrated in the coastal plain of eastern North Carolina, during the 1880s and 1890s an increasing percentage of black firms were locating in the piedmont (table 19).

Although entrance into this region marked a new trend for black businessmen in the 1880s and 1890s, there was a large degree of continuity even in this process. Like black businessmen in the coastal plain counties both before and after 1880, the black businessmen in the piedmont tended to locate in communities that had a higher percentage of blacks than those counties in the same section that had no black enterprises (table 19).[25] Therefore, it was not surprising that Green Oliver opened his general store in Caswell County, which in 1880 was one of only two piedmont counties with a black majority population (59.8%).

Success was not assured to those piedmont black businessmen who tried to locate their new firms in markets that had not been carved out by other black entrepreneurs. In fact, because black customers in this region for years had had no choice but to patronize white businessmen, the piedmont initially was a region where black firms remained active in business for only a short period (table 18). During the 1880s, a decade in which black businessmen fared much worse than they had during the 1870s, those who had located in the piedmont failed much faster than those in the coastal plain. On the whole, black piedmont entrepreneurs were only about one-third as likely to survive in business for the decade as their coastal plain counterparts. Their relative rate of success only worsened during the second half of the decade.[26]

If during the 1880s black piedmont businessmen establishing a foothold encountered difficulty, their fortunes improved markedly during the 1890s. In fact, during that decade they were slightly more likely to remain in business than coastal plain black firms (table 18). As a result of their relatively new-found success, there was a surge in the number of black firms in the piedmont. During the 1890s the number of black firms grew six times faster in the piedmont than in the coastal plain (table 19).[27]

The disparity in the regional growth of black firms during the 1890s in part resulted from the fact that the black population in the piedmont increased twice as fast as that in the coastal plain.[28] In addition, the decennial growth in the number of piedmont black firms had a very localized character. The number of black businesses in just two cities, Winston and Charlotte, leaped from 2 to 29 between 1890 and 1900. This surge in black entrepreneurship resulted from the needs of the burgeoning black populations of these two communities, which by 1900 totaled 12,194 residents. Black residents of these expanding cities were entirely dependent on mercantile firms for their basic daily necessities. Thus, in 1900 more than half of the black credit-rated firms in these two cities were groceries and general stores.

The piedmont boom of the 1890s could not be sustained during the early years of the next century. During the first decade of the twentieth century the postwar regional demographic trend reversed itself as the black population of the coastal plain actually grew at twice the rate of the black population in the piedmont.[29] Indeed, during these years the number of black firms in the piedmont actually declined, while the coastal plain experienced continual growth. This decline probably resulted from too many blacks' having located in the piedmont in the previous two decades. Indicative of this overgrowth of black firms, black businessmen in the coastal plain were nearly twice as likely as those in the piedmont to survive from 1900 to 1910 than those of the piedmont (table 18).

Besides creating businesses in the piedmont and the coastal plain, black businessmen slowly ventured into the mountain region in western North Carolina after 1880. Their attempt to create new markets in this

Table 20. Black Proportion of County Population with and without
Black Credit-Rated Firms by Region, 1890 and 1900

	Counties with Firms in		Counties without Firms in	
	1890	1900	1890	1900
Coastal plain	49.4%	47.4%	41.2%	38.3%
Piedmont	32.2	30.5	20.3	20.9
Mountain	17.3	16.6	6.6	6.1
Total	40.5	38.7	22.8	19.3

Source: Mercantile Agency Reference Book, 1890 and 1900, Library of Congress,
Washington DC.

section of the state was even riskier than their movement into the piedmont since traditionally few blacks resided in this region. Like black businessmen in both the coastal plain and the piedmont, those in the mountain region established their firms in communities where the percentage
of the population that was black was higher than the percentage in the
region as a whole (table 20). Hence by 1885 a black general store,
Chas. E. Lowe & Co., and a black grocery, John W. Woodward, had been
established in Asheville, in Buncombe County, and in Morganton, in
Burke County, respectively. Although blacks constituted a small minority
in these two counties in 1900, their share of the population was well
above the regional average.[30]

The relatively disproportionate black population in Buncombe and
Burke Counties did not ensure that the black mountain businessmen
would experience success. Indeed, neither of the black firms established
in 1885 was still in business in 1890. Moreover, the two new black firms
that had been created in Asheville and Morganton by 1890, Swan Green-
ley and A. Moore, both blacksmiths, had closed their doors permanently
by 1900.

Even though black businessmen did not flourish in the mountains
during the late nineteenth century, the continuing growth of the black
population in this region, especially in Asheville, created a larger market
for blacks who were willing to assume the risk of establishing firms.[31] In
1900 there were three black businessmen in Asheville: Isaac Dixon and
Henry Doster, both grocers, and A. R. Leatherwood, a dyer. Dixon and

Doster, as well as the other black firm in the region, J. P. Aiken, a grocer in the village of Brevard, in Transylvania County, would survive in business until 1905 and Dixon would last at least until 1910.

Although the credit-rated black business community in North Carolina grew more geographically diverse after 1880 as it spread largely from the coastal plain into both the piedmont and the mountain areas, it became somewhat more economically narrow as its members increasingly focused their efforts in the mercantile sector of the economy (table 21). Although this trend was not entirely linear, between 1880 and 1905 the share of the black firms devoted to this type of endeavor grew from about half to three-quarters, largely because of the number of black businessmen who were meeting the needs of the growing black urban population. Hence, whereas in 1880 the ratio between black general stores (which generally served rural and small-town customers) and black groceries (whose clientele tended to be more urban) was 3 to 1, by 1905 there were two general stores for every three groceries.[32] Indeed, reflecting the needs of their urban customers, some of the black mercantile firms during this period were becoming specialized, for example, selling only green groceries or meat.

The second most evident trend among black credit-rated firms was the decline of blacks in the liquor trade. Although in both 1885 and

Table 21. Type of Credit-Rated Black Firms, 1875–1905

Type of Firm	1875 (N = 56)	1880 (N = 83)	1885 (N = 164)	1890 (N = 200)	1900 (N = 268)	1905 (N = 316)
Mercantile	58.9%	53.0%	43.3%	52.5%	70.1%	76.6%
Skilled	16.1	22.9	22.6	18.5	12.7	10.8
Liquor	12.5	6.0	9.1	7.5	3.7	.3
Mercantile-liquor	3.6	6.0	6.7	4.5	3.4	2.5
Confection/ confection-liquor	5.4	1.2	7.3	3.0	0	.3
Diversified	0	2.4	1.2	3.5	1.5	3.5
Other	0	6.0	1.2	2.5	1.9	1.3
Service	3.6	2.4	8.5	8.0	6.7	4.7

Source: Mercantile Agency Reference Book, 1875, 1880, 1885, 1890, 1900, 1905, Library of Congress, Washington DC.

Note: Only firms headed by men are included.

1890 there were 15 black liquor stores, bars, or saloons, by 1905 there was but a single black firm devoted exclusively to the sale of liquor. A number of firms still sold liquor, but largely only in conjunction with the mercantile trade. However, even these types of firms were declining as a share of all black businesses.

Although blacks did not cease their involvement in the liquor trade by choice, racial motivation seems to have played a smaller role in impeding blacks from earning a living from the sale of alcohol in this period than in the mid 1870s, when many black bars and saloons were driven out of business after the Democrats used the state legislature to alter local governments. Despite a slight resurgence of black involvement in the liquor trade during the early and mid 1880s, for the rest of that decade and throughout the 1890s towns throughout the state began to tighten their regulations regarding liquor sales. These measures were supported by many black leaders in the state, and a very active black Good Templars movement advocated prohibition. However, since the laws passed in 1903 and 1905 extending prohibition to all rural communities and the popular vote that ended all liquor sales in the state by 1910 all occurred soon after most blacks lost the franchise, it is impossible to determine to what degree the majority of blacks favored these measures. There is little doubt that the law that finally introduced prohibition statewide could not have come about without the support of the Democratic Party, which since the end of the Civil War had never shown itself to be a friend of black businessmen, especially blacks involved in the liquor trade.[33]

At the same time that certain black businessmen in North Carolina were losing their opportunity to conduct their firms, another group of black entrepreneurs, black businesswomen, began to establish a record of achievement. The number of credit-rated firms headed by women grew from two in 1885 to four in 1890 and six in 1900. The number had fallen off slightly by 1905, when it stood at five. The 13 female entrepreneurs who ran credit-rated firms in these years largely mirrored their male counterparts. More than four-fifths resided in the coastal plain, the other 2 in the piedmont. Because few women acquired skilled trades, as entrepreneurs they focused on mercantile businesses. Eleven conducted groceries or general stores, one ran a combination restaurant and bar, and one ran a confectionery.[34]

It would be interesting to compare women's and men's ability to maintain their businesses over time, but such a comparison is complicated by two problems. First, because the number of women conducting businesses at any one point in time was too small, we cannot make a valid comparison between their success rate and that of men. Second, if a woman married, her firm might falsely appear to have failed simply because a change in her surname would make it impossible for us to continue tracing her enterprise. Despite these problems, there is some reason to believe that businesswomen may have succeeded at a rate comparable to that of men. From 1890 to 1900 the percentage of firms conducted by women that remained active was the same as the percentage of firms conducted by men. In fact, from 1900 to 1905 the success rate for women markedly exceeded that of men.[35] One woman, Martha Copeland, was able to keep her general store in Winfall, in Perquimans County, open for business for at least seventeen years during this period, an accomplishment matched by few black or white men.

The limited information about black businesswomen also suggests that most of them were married or widowed.[36] For example, the names of three of the five women in 1905 were preceded by the title "Mrs.," and often the women's husbands' first names, rather than the women's own, were followed by this title. Many of the women probably had not initiated these firms but continued to run them after their husbands died or shifted to another occupation. For example, in 1900 Mrs. William A. Reed, of Winfall, was running a general store, the same trade her husband had conducted since at least 1880. That it was often the case that firms run by women had been created by their husbands explains how these women could have run mercantile firms, which generally demanded a level of capital that was beyond the reach of most black women.

Despite its broadening geographic distribution and the slight change in its gender composition, in two very important respects—in the structure of firms and their degree of success—the black business community experienced more continuity than change from 1880 until after the turn of the century. Black firms overwhelmingly remained single proprietorships during this period, just as they had from 1865 to 1879. The share of black firms composed of only one individual in 1905 was nearly identical to the share in the immediate postwar years.[37] This continuity occurred largely because mercantile firms, which had been the type of firm most likely to be run by more than one entrepreneur during the Reconstruction years, increasingly were run by only a single entrepreneur.[38] The decline in this pattern may have come about because enough individual blacks had accumulated the necessary assets by the end of the century to run a successful grocery or general store without having to pool their funds with another businessman.

Slightly countervailing this trend among black merchants was the tendency of skilled black tradesmen during this period to bring in partners, probably to meet the costs of renting or buying property in the growing urban black business community. And many skilled businessmen were conducting their firms with relatives. For example, in 1905 five of the eight firms run by men in partnership with their sons were the firms of skilled tradesmen.

The other area in which credit-rated black firms demonstrated continuity was their ability to remain in business (table 18). After falling drastically during the 1880s from the exceptionally high level of the 1870s, the persistence rate of black firms experienced a slow but steady improvement during each decade through 1910.

Despite this continual improvement, the success rate of black firms varied considerably depending on the size of the community in which the businesses were located (table 22). From 1870 to 1910 the likelihood of firms staying active for more than a decade was lowest in hamlets and villages, communities with fewer than 1,000 inhabitants. Such communities probably had too few customers to keep a black entrepreneur in business, especially since whites generally made up half of the population in these communities and the local white competition likely had been in business longer and possessed larger assets.

Although medium and large towns and cities, communities with more than 2,499 residents, generally provided better economic environments for black firms than did hamlets and villages, certain problems kept them from being the most attractive locations for a black businessmen who desired to remain in business very long. Although cities provided

Table 22. Decennial Rates of Persistence of Credit-Rated Black Firms by Size of Community, 1870–1910

	Hamlets and Villages	*Small Towns*	*Medium and Large Towns and Cities*
1870–80	16.6%	50.0%	83.3%
1880–90	17.6	37.5	14.7
1890–1900	17.9	29.1	26.5
1900–1910	25.6	47.5	27.3
Total	21.6	37.2	26.7

Source: Mercantile Agency Reference Book, 1870, 1880, 1890, 1900, 1910, Library of Congress, Washington DC.

Note: Size of community is defined as follows: hamlets and villages, less than 1,000; small towns, 1,000–2,499; medium and large towns and cities, more than 2,500.

black firms, especially general stores and groceries, a large clientele, the costs of running such firms in larger communities would have been high because of higher rents and property values. Further, if black firms were extending their customers credit, the risks may have been much higher in larger communities, where it would have been more difficult to gauge the credit-worthiness of the rapidly growing black population.

Except during the immediate postwar years, black firms fared best in small towns, communities with 1,000 to 2,499 residents. The problems of smaller and larger communities simply were less severe in small towns, where there were enough customers to sustain a business and it was not too difficult to find out whether clients would be able to pay their bills.

The community of Weldon, in Halifax County, was a typical small town where black firms encountered their greatest success. By 1885, when Weldon had 1,000 residents, William Anderson had created a general store there. Although Anderson seems never to have accumulated substantial assets, he kept his store open until at least 1900. His accomplishment was even the more remarkable because by 1890 he had been joined in Weldon by another black businessman, William Smith, who conducted a combination grocery and liquor establishment. Smith also survived in business at least fifteen years. By 1900 two other combination grocery and liquor firms had been created in Weldon, and both remained open for at least a decade. Given the imminent loss of the liquor trade, this achievement was impressive.

Although black firms in Weldon may have been unusually successful because the small town had a majority black population, communities with a similar racial composition but whose populations were substantially larger or smaller did not provide black firms with as healthy an economic environment. For example, the hamlet of Louisburg, which also had a black majority population, was simply too small to allow any black firm to last through either the 1880s or the 1890s. Likewise, at the other end of the scale, New Bern, whose black population composed nearly two-thirds of its 6,000 inhabitants in 1880, only sustained 1 of its 9 black firms in business until 1890. Between 1890 and 1900, a period in which the community's black population grew to 5,878, only 4 of New Bern's 15 black firms remained open.

Although there was no such thing as a typical small town that contained a typical black businessman, the experience of York Garrett of Tarboro during the late nineteenth and early twentieth centuries indicates the level of success a black businessman could achieve in a small town.[39] York Garrett was born a slave on 5 July 1859 in Washington County. Little is known about his parents, both of whom were slaves, except that his father, a harnessmaker, ran away when York was five years old and was never heard from again.

How, when, or why York made his way to Tarboro, a community with about two thousand residents, about half of whom were black, is not known. What is known is that by the 1880s he had worked in two different Tarboro stores owned by whites. Sometime during the late 1880s the owner of the second store asked York, in whom he had substantial confidence, if he was interested in purchasing the firm's stock on payments. York took advantage of this opportunity even though he knew that it would take many years to pay off the debt. In fact, he did not make the final payment until 1901. Throughout this period York had not only to pay off his obligation but also to meet a rent of about $40 a month for the building.

In order to preserve his business during its infancy, in 1895 York sold a half-interest in the store to another black, Henry Cherry. This partnership continued for only about three years and was dissolved not for economic but for political reasons. York, who had always been very interested in politics, had been elected a justice of the peace in Edgecombe County. When he decided to run for a seat in the North Carolina house of representatives in 1898, however, Cherry, for unknown reasons, refused to support his candidacy. York failed to win the office, and he never again took on a business partner.[40]

To minimize his overhead costs, York relocated his business a number of times, in different buildings in Tarboro and in the neighboring black community of Princeville.[41] He finally settled down in 1904, when he could afford to buy his own store on the first block of Main Street in Tarboro. Before purchasing his own building in 1904, York carried liquor as well as groceries in his store. Thereafter he had to stop selling liquor because of the new prohibition law.

York obtained most of his supplies from local white wholesalers who trusted him enough to extend him credit on his purchases. In turn, he extended credit to about half of his customers, all of whom were blacks living in the immediate vicinity of Tarboro. York had received enough education to be able to read and write; therefore, he could record these credit purchases in ledgers. Those customers who were farmers occasionally paid their debts to York with products they had grown.

Besides maintaining his store and taking part in politics, York was very active in fraternal societies. Not only was he a member of the Odd Fellows and the Knights of Pythias but by 1908 he held the second highest office in the Mount Lebanon Masonic lodge.[42] Apparently his participation in these lodges consumed so many evenings each week that it upset

his wife. It is difficult to determine whether his membership in these
lodges improved York's standing in Tarboro or confirmed the status he
already had attained. Recalling his father's participation in these lodges,
York's youngest son was convinced that his father's various memberships
were an indication that people "looked up" to him and considered him
one of the "outstanding people" in the community.

York's economic success matched the level of social respect he gained.
At one time he owned at least six houses in Tarboro and Princeville, most
of which he rented to blacks. In addition, he was able to send at least
three of his children to college. Finally, when he died, in 1928, he left
each of his children a house. The day after he died, the local white newspaper described York as "one of Tarboro's most worthy and respected
Colored citizens." [43]

Although credit ratings reveal some general patterns of black entrepreneurship throughout North Carolina during the fifty years after the Civil
War, starting about 1900 city directories provide many other valuable
clues about the status of black firms located in urban communities. Before 1900, directories were compiled only for some of the largest cities
in the eastern part of the state, and then only infrequently. By the turn
of the century, in part reflecting the substantial growth of the piedmont
communities and of Asheville in the mountains, many more directories
were compiled for additional cities.

Directories published around 1915 for 19 diverse North Carolina
communities reveal some general trends concerning the types of firms
blacks businessmen were conducting at this time. These communities
varied considerably in size, racial composition, and location. Based on
their population in 1910, their populations ranged from as few as 4,599
residents (Statesville) to as many as 34,762 (Charlotte); the median
population was 8,051 (Rocky Mount). Collectively, they had a black
population of 36.3 percent; however, the black population of the individual communities ranged from as low as 10.2 percent (Burlington) to
as high as 56.7 percent (New Bern). Eleven of the communities were
located in the piedmont, and seven in the coastal plain; Asheville was the
only mountain community with a city directory at this time.

Although blacks in fact operated 93 different types of businesses, only
the 39 types in which at least 19 total firms (both black and white) were
engaged are noted (table 23). These firms account for the vast majority
of all black firms.[44] There was quite a range in the percentage of types of
firms operated by each race, from midwifing, which blacks dominated,
to boarding houses, which whites dominated. Because the black share of
the population in these communities ranged from 44.3 percent in the

Table 23. Types of Black Firms Noted in City Directories by Region, 1909–16

Type of Firm	Number of Black Firms	Number of Total Firms	Percent of Firms Black	Percentage of Firms Operated by Blacks in		
				Coastal Plain	Mountain	Piedmont
Midwifing	32	32	100.0%	100.0%	none	100.0%
Eating house	195	213	91.5	99.0	66.7	91.9
Hack or cab service	27	30	90.0	100.0	66.7	94.4
Hairdressing	25	29	86.2	100.0	87.5	83.3
Barbering	199	369	53.9	75.6	34.3	43.3
Draying	71	141	50.4	71.4	40.6	44.6
Cleaning or pressing	132	270	48.9	60.8	64.3	41.1
Funeral directing	12	25	48.0	56.2	0.0	33.3
Dye works	11	23	47.8	0.0	50.0	47.4
Shoemaking or repair	100	221	45.2	54.7	31.8	41.9
Soft-drink selling	32	72	44.4	52.3	100.0	29.6
Undertaking	11	25	44.0	37.5	40.0	50.0
Blacksmithing	45	111	40.5	55.9	10.0	37.3
House painting	8	24	33.3	71.4	10.0	28.6
Wood or coal dealing	26	78	33.3	34.5	20.0	34.1
Billiard or pool room	18	59	30.5	77.8	30.8	18.9
Tailoring	50	183	27.3	45.4	25.5	18.8
Dressmaking	40	151	26.5	51.5	15.4	21.5
Watchmaking	7	27	25.9	33.3	0.0	20.0
Photographing	18	72	25.0	10.5	10.0	34.9
Cigar and tobacco selling	6	25	24.0	0.0	0.0	24.0
Music teaching	9	43	20.9	22.2	4.8	100.0
Furnished rooms	6	29	20.7	33.3	11.1	37.5
Retail grocery	345	1,775	19.4	25.9	9.4	17.0
Theater	6	31	19.4	18.2	0.0	20.0
Hotel	6	33	18.2	0.0	0.0	18.2
Drug store	35	204	17.2	17.9	5.3	18.6
Confectionery	15	89	16.8	20.0	0.0	14.3

Table 23. *Continued*

Type of Firm	Number of Black Firms	Number of Total Firms	Percent of Firms Black	Percentage of Firms Operated by Blacks in		
				Coastal Plain	Mountain	Piedmont
Livery stable	5	30	16.7	15.4	0.0	17.6
Meat market	24	150	16.0	25.0	9.1	10.3
Dry-goods store	3	19	15.8	12.5	0.0	33.3
Printery	4	27	14.8	13.3	0.0	16.7
Millinery	6	42	14.3	23.5	0.0	8.0
Contracting	12	96	12.5	17.4	0.0	10.9
General merchandising	11	90	12.2	12.8	0.0	11.8
Restaurant	5	48	10.4	11.8	0.0	9.7
Dentistry	11	114	9.6	15.4	0.0	6.7
Real-estate seller	18	279	6.4	9.1	7.9	4.3
Boardinghouse	24	379	6.3	4.0	5.4	8.6
Total	1,610	5,658	28.4	36.7	20.2	25.2

Sources: City directories of Asheville, 1916; Burlington, 1909; Charlotte, 1915; Concord, 1916; Durham, 1915; Fayetteville, 1915; Gastonia, 1910; Greensboro, 1915; High Point, 1910; New Bern, 1916; Raleigh, 1915; Rocky Mount, 1912; Salisbury, 1915; Statesville, 1916; Washington, 1916; Wilmington, 1915; Wilson, 1916; and Winston-Salem, 1915. For a full citation for each city directory, see the bibliography.

Note: The 39 types of firms in table 23 comprised 5,658 (95.3%) of the 5,934 black firms listed in these directories.

coastal plain communities to 32.3 percent in the piedmont to 28.6 percent in the mountains, generally coastal plain blacks controlled a larger share of each type of firm than their counterparts in the other two regions. Despite this factor, what is most striking is that blacks tended to dominate or be underrepresented in the same types of firms in all three regions.

The reason why the black share of certain types of firms was fairly consistent throughout the state most likely is related to the costs of operating these firms. For example, while overall blacks conducted 28.4 percent of all firms in these cities, they only controlled 18.8 percent of mercantile firms, which generally were among the most expensive types of firms to initiate and maintain because of the high urban rents and the

amount of stock they needed to keep on hand. By contrast, blacks operated 35.1 percent of all skilled trades and 33.3 percent of all service-
related firms. Their share of the skilled and service sector would have
been even higher had not some of these firms, such as theaters, hotels,
livery stables, print shops, building contractors, restaurants, real-estate
firms, and boarding houses, tended to require high capital-investment
costs. Blacks often operated firms that required the same kinds of skills
as those demanded by firms with high-entry costs but required less capital. For example, although they conducted very few restaurants, blacks
operated nearly all of the smaller eating houses. Similarly, although few
blacks could afford the costs of running a full-service livery stable, many
could afford the one or two horses necessary to maintain hacks or cabs
or to provide drayage service.

Racial discrimination clearly played a role in the types of firms blacks
operated. Black funeral directors and undertakers were largely guaran-
teed a high percentage of the business of black clients, whom white firms
generally would not serve. Other types of firms that traditionally had
been relegated to blacks, such as barbering, continued to be so.

If blacks were often underrepresented in certain trades, there is no
evidence that they were completely barred from these or other endeavors statewide. For example, in 1915 there were no black-operated restaurants in Durham. However, 30 miles away, in Raleigh, there were two
such firms: the Ideal Cafe & Lunch Room and the Raleigh Cafe. Likewise, although Raleigh did not have a black-operated livery firm, Peyton
Smith of Durham provided such a service. Although these and similar
cases do not prove that racism more than economics was the root cause
of why certain communities had few or no black firms in specific sectors
of the economy, it does suggest that blacks who wanted to run a particular business could find some community, usually within the same region,
where they could do so.

This new level of entrepreneurship extended to black women as well
as to black men. At least 17.2 percent of all black firms in these communities were conducted by women. Black women generally dominated
firms that served a largely female clientele: dressmaking (95.0%), hair-
dressing (72.0%), midwifing (68.8%). Like most black men engaged in
business, black women tended to focus their efforts in areas where less
expensive alternatives were available. For example, although no black
women ran hotels, they controlled nearly two-thirds (63.3%) of furnished rooms and boarding houses combined. And although no black
women operated restaurants, they ran 17.4 percent of the eating houses.
Although they were underrepresented in enterprises that required a high
amount of capital, black women did run such endeavors. For example,

6.7 percent of black-operated retail grocery stores were conducted by women. Even a few black women in the state worked in those types of firms that traditionally were controlled by men. For example, Holly Haid of Asheville ran a hack firm, June Peebles of Durham was a shoemaker, and Della Evans of Salisbury operated a billiard and pool room.

Although the city directories from around 1915 reveal a great deal about the types of firms blacks operated statewide at that time, we would learn more from looking at trends in the black business community in these same cities over time. Wilmington, however, was the only city for which a directory was compiled on a fairly continuous basis from the end of the Civil War until 1915. But Wilmington's business environment for blacks may not have been entirely typical for two reasons. First, the black portion of the city's population declined from 58.9 percent in 1870 to 47.0 in 1910. Second, in November 1898 the city experienced a race riot that culminated in the murder of 11 blacks and the wounding of 25 and led to the exodus of a number of the leading black political and business leaders.[45]

Despite these problems, the black business community in Wilmington fared quite well during this period. The Wilmington city directories reveal that except for a very slight downturn in the late 1880s and the early 1890s the share of black firms in the city gradually increased from 17.0 percent in 1875 to 20.6 percent in 1885, 20.4 percent in 1895, 28.2 percent in 1905, and 31.7 percent in 1915.[46] Moreover, the types of firms blacks operated in the city increased in number. Whereas blacks ran only 10 types of firms in 1875, by 1895 that number had risen to 24, and in 1915 it was 29. Further, blacks were beginning to operate firms in areas that had been exclusively white. In 1895 there were 18 types of firms that were operated by whites but not by blacks. Over the next twenty years blacks initiated firms in all but 5 of those areas. In 4 of the areas in which they failed to make inroads this failure may have resulted from economic rather than racial factors as the capital requirements of those enterprises—brokering, commission merchandising, dry goods, and hardware—were relatively high. The fifth area, wholesale liquor dealings, simply disappeared for whites as well as for blacks because of prohibition. Finally, in the mercantile sector black businessmen seem to have fared especially well in the city. The number of black grocers in the city grew fourfold from 1895 to 1915, and the percentage of all groceries run by blacks rose from 10.6 percent to 20.1 percent. Hence, Wilmington, which we might have expected to hold few prospects for black firms, in fact provided a relatively attractive business environment.

The attractiveness of this business environment also extended to Wilmington's black women. Paralleling the statewide development of a female urban black business community, Wilmington witnessed a surge in the number of women entrepreneurs with the new century. As late as 1895 there had been only two black women running firms in the city: Mrs. Eliza Borden, keeper of a boarding house, and Mrs. R. A. Sneed, a butcher. These two women's enterprises represented only 2.7 percent of the black-operated firms in the city. By 1915 black women were running 33 firms (16.2% of all black firms) of eight different types. Although most of these women operated businesses in which women generally dominated the market because of low entrance costs (dressmaking and midwifing), three women operated firms that required relatively higher amounts of capital (retail groceries).

The city directories of other communities during the ten years preceding 1915 also reveal that black businesses were steadily growing despite the political setbacks blacks were experiencing. This growth was most evident in the emerging cities of the piedmont, where black entrepreneurs competed with a flourishing white business community. Between 1905 and 1915, in three piedmont cities—Durham, Greensboro, and Winston-Salem—the number of black firms grew from 225 to 463 and the portion of all firms operated by blacks grew from 23.7 percent to 28.4 percent.[47] The black share of these firms increased even though from 1900 to 1910 the black proportion of the population of the three communities dropped slightly, from 39.0 percent to 38.1 percent. Further, from 1905 to 1915 the scope of the black business community was broadening: the number of types of firms in which blacks were engaged grew from 28 to 31 in Durham, 18 to 25 in Greensboro, and 14 to 46 in Winston-Salem. At the same time, black businessmen in these cities also made significant strides in entering what had previously been all-white endeavors. For example, whereas in 1905 all 20 of Winston-Salem's general-merchandise firms were run by whites, by 1915 5 of the 37 firms were operated by blacks. In 1905 Greensboro had no hotels operated by blacks to complement the six run by whites. By 1915 there were two run by blacks and nine run by whites.

Starting in 1865 from a few firms clustered in the eastern part of North Carolina that had antebellum roots, by 1915 the black business community had extended itself across the state and into new sectors of the economy. What stands out is that despite two national depressions, a restrictive local and state political environment, a relatively limited and disadvantaged clientele, adverse demographic factors, and even the sometimes inhibiting circumstances resulting from the exceptional success of a limited number of black firms, black entrepreneurship experienced widespread and diverse success during these years.

3

Collective Efforts toward Enterprise

IN 1915 Berry O'Kelly, speaking before the National Negro Business League's annual convention in Boston, provided a personal testimonial about the success he had experienced as a black businessman in North Carolina. O'Kelly's story was typical of the rags-to-riches stories that were commonly presented at the National Negro Business League's conventions and that Americans of this era enjoyed hearing. O'Kelly described how he had overcome one adversity after another.[1] Not only had he been born a slave near the outset of the Civil War in Orange County, North Carolina, but his mother had died shortly after his birth. Raised by her relatives in the black village of Method, near Raleigh, in Wake County, O'Kelly had proved to be an industrious individual. While in his twenties, he had worked himself up from clerk to partner and later to sole owner of a store in Method. In 1890 he had been fortunate to become the postmaster at Method, which meant that whites and blacks would have to come into his store to pick up their mail. Later he had created an investment firm, organized a shoe company, and leased space to black-operated businesses in an office building that he had built in downtown Raleigh. In addition, he had become actively involved in real estate, life insurance, a black newspaper, and banking. By the time he addressed the National Negro Business League he was said to have accumulated an estate worth "no less than $75,000." In his 1915 speech he noted that as a black entrepreneur he had "no trouble getting any money he wanted from banks." When he died 16 years later, during the

7. Berry O'Kelly. (Courtesy of North Carolina Division of
Archives and History, N76.11.41)

Depression, despite the decline in property values during that era his
real estate alone was valued at $145,855.

Although O'Kelly's achievements as a black businessman were note-
worthy, his speech before the National Negro Business League reveals
much about the nature of black economic success during this era. O'Kelly
would have been the first to admit that individual and family efforts did
not assure blacks economic success. His career demonstrated how collective efforts toward enterprise and institutions played an essential role in
promoting black economic success. In addition to having a life membership in the National Negro Business League, O'Kelly belonged to, and

served on, the state executive committees of both the black Masons and the Odd Fellows. Further, he served as president of the North Carolina Industrial Association and devoted much time and money to numerous charitable and educational endeavors to improve the lives of blacks.

Although many black fraternal orders were created in North Carolina after the Civil War, none was as influential in fostering black economic advancement as the Prince Hall Freemasons. Black Masons date the beginning of their organization in America to 1775, when an Irish regiment stationed in Boston with the British forces initiated 15 free blacks into its lodge.[2] After the troops left Boston during the Revolutionary War, this lodge, now made up only of blacks, was called African Lodge No. 459. Nine years later the Mother Grand Lodge of England issued the lodge a formal charter. Prince Hall, the master of the lodge in Boston, went on to organize other black Masonic lodges in Philadelphia and Providence, Rhode Island. After Hall's death in 1807, black Masonry, or, as it is termed, Prince Hall Freemasonry, continued to grow.

Shortly after the end of the Civil War the first black Masonic lodge in North Carolina, King Solomon Lodge, was created in New Bern.[3] Within five years 3 other lodges had been organized in Wilmington, Fayetteville, and Raleigh.[4] On 1 March 1870 these 4 lodges convened in Wilmington and organized the Most Worshipful Grand Lodge of the State of North Carolina. During the next decade black Masonry experienced remarkable growth in North Carolina as the 4 lodges, with 181 members in 1870, expanded to 37 lodges and 1,085 members by 1880. During the 1880s the pace of growth slowed, probably as a result of the poor economic conditions and the large exodus of blacks out of the state during the latter part of this decade. Still, by 1890 there were 59 lodges and 1,231 members. The 1890s was a much healthier decade for the order: by 1900 there were 90 lodges and 2,037 members. The first decade of the new century witnessed exceptional growth, with 358 lodges and more than 10,000 members by 1910. That year 300 communities in the state had at least one lodge, and some of the larger cities had a number of them.

During its infancy North Carolina black Masonry clearly had an elite character. For example, 11 men who were members in 1870 either had already served or would eventually serve in the state legislature.[5] One member, John A. Hyman, of Warren County, had been a delegate to the state constitutional convention in 1868 and a state senator and shortly would be elected to the U.S. House of Representatives. And many members who never served in the legislature held other significant municipal and county positions. For example, James Lowrey, the prominent Wilmington black carriage maker, would be both an alderman and an election judge. Likewise, Thomas Lomax, of the Eureka Lodge in Fayetteville, served on the Cumberland County Commission.

Another indication of the elite character of the Masonic members during the fraternal society's formative years is that more than one-fourth of them owned real estate, about four times the state average for blacks in 1870. In the Giblem Lodge, in Wilmington, more than half the members were landowners. Further, some of the Wilmington Masons were among the wealthiest blacks in their community. For example, William J. Kellogg Jr., a wheelwright, owned real estate valued at $3,000. In 1860 he had been a free black landowner in Wilmington. Another sign of their status is that more than half of the Masons who were landowners were mulattoes.[6] Fewer than one-tenth of the members who owned land were laborers. The vast majority were skilled tradesmen and merchants. Given the urban character of the communities where lodges were first located, very few of the Masons were farmers, and even for those few, farming may have been only a secondary occupation.[7]

Once Masonic lodges began to be founded in rural locations, black farmers became members. However, those black farmers who were early members of the order differed from the vast majority of blacks who worked on the land. For example, in the first rural lodge, Rising Sun Lodge, in the village of Horseshoe in Columbus County, 9 of the 13 who were members during the first year of the lodge owned real estate.

In addition to the fact that black Masons tended to own land, there also was a close relationship between black Masonry and black economic enterprise in North Carolina. Although every black businessman did not join the fraternal order and every member of a lodge was not an entrepreneur, there was a strong correlation between the two. Scholars have long noted the role membership in voluntary associations, and particularly Masonry, played in promoting a member's economic progress. By increasing one's personal and business contacts and signifying individual moral discipline, Masonic membership enhanced a businessman's chances of receiving the credit that was necessary for success.[8] Therefore, it is not surprising that new Masonic lodges often were formed in communities where black businessmen were receiving credit ratings.[9] In 1870 three of the four communities where black businessmen had already been credit-rated had black Masonic lodges. By 1880 there were black Masonic lodges in three-fifths of the communities with credit-rated black businessmen, and in some of the remaining 15 communities black businessmen would be credit-rated within a few years or such businessmen already resided in the county but within another community.[10]

There is clear evidence that these black entrepreneurs played a significant role in the organization of these lodges. For example, during the mid 1870s both Lewis H. Fisher and Wiley Lowrey had opened general stores in the town of Kinston, in Lenoir County. In 1880 Fisher served as the secretary and Lowrey was the treasurer of Kinston's recently formed King David Lodge. During the 1880s three other credit-rated black businessmen in Kinston served as officers of the lodge: J. C. Hargett and E. W. Borden, both of whom were grocers, and P. R. Borden, a confectioner. Again, not every black businessman of stature joined the order. For example, one of Kinston's preeminent black businessmen, Charles F. Dunn, who for many years conducted a general store and later opened a bank, never appeared on King David Lodge's membership roll. Perhaps he belonged to one of the other types of lodges in Kinston.[11]

Although prominent black businessmen and landowning farmers played a fundamental role during Masonry's first two decades, thereafter the character of lodge membership was bound to change. This was especially true from 1890 to 1910, when the membership grew nearly tenfold as new lodges were created in some of the smallest villages, hamlets, and crossroads throughout the state. The economic status of lodge members shifted during the 1890s; a sample of five lodges shows a decline in the share of members who owned real estate from one-third to one-fourth.[12] This decline in status occurred during years when the percentage of blacks who owned land increased statewide.

In addition to the decline in the economic status of the Mason membership, there was a fairly constant turnover in membership and leadership. By 1910 the median number of members per lodge was 28; however, 127 lodges had fewer than 20 members, and 16 had fewer than 10. The smallest lodge had only 3 members. Since each lodge was supposed to have 12 officers, many lodges were actually too small to fill every office. Hence, in the smaller lodges any member could become an officer as long as he remained in the organization for a few years. However, few members seem to have continued their lodge involvement over a long period. In the Giblem Lodge in Wilmington, for example, just over half of the original members remained members during the 1890s. Only 2 of those who were officers in 1890 were still officers by 1900. In fact, 5 of the 12 who were officers in 1900 had not even been members a decade earlier. A similar turnover took place in the Doric Lodge, in Durham, during the 1890s. Only about two-fifths of the lodge's members stayed in the lodge during the whole decade, and 7 of its 12 officers in 1900 had not been members in 1890.[13]

The influx of so many new members appears to have played a major role in lowering the overall economic status of lodge members, as newer members tended to be less affluent than older ones. Only about one-third of the new members of the Giblem and Doric Lodges owned real estate, compared with nearly half of the old members.[14]

Despite signs that there was some decline in the economic status of Masons, the order's doors would remain closed to many blacks for financial reasons. Besides the high moral standing that individuals applying for membership had to demonstrate, membership fees probably were the greatest barrier for prospective members. In addition to an initial $2.50 membership fee, every member was required to pay monthly membership dues, which generally ranged from a quarter to a half-dollar.[15] Although there are no records indicating how many men were denied membership because they could not pay these fees, every year a significant percentage of Masons was excluded from continued membership for nonpayment of their dues. In 1880, a year in which there were 1,085 members in the order statewide, 137 members were excluded for nonpayment of dues. In some lodges a substantial share of the members were cited for nonpayment. For example, in 1880 the Mount Moriah Lodge, in South Mills, excluded two-fifths of its members for not paying their dues.[16] Many of these members would eventually pay their back dues and again become members in good standing. Except for temporary exclusion from good standing, there appears to have been no stigma attached to the inability to pay dues. In fact, one of the members cited for not paying dues in 1880 was serving as an officer of the Mount Moriah Lodge in 1890. However, many Masons who could not continue to fulfill the financial commitment they had agreed to on joining their lodge had to cease their membership. If many of these men who had been admitted had to leave their lodges for financial reasons, clearly the cost of membership would have been initially prohibitive for many, if not most, blacks.

Although membership fees served as a barrier for many blacks who desired to become Masons, by the turn of the century hundreds of new blacks annually were able to meet the costs of membership and share in the benefits of the fraternal order. One of the major benefits of this membership, especially for those individuals interested in increasing their financial status, was that the lodges provided them with experience in property management. Although each lodge usually had a finance committee, the other members often were called upon to make a number of decisions concerning the maintenance of the lodge's property. For example, on 10 January 1876 the Excelsior Lodge, in Raleigh, convened with the black Good Templars, who shared the lodge hall, for the purpose of discussing a venture in which each member would pay $5 in order to pay off the mortgage on the lodge property. Likewise, on 28 February 1881 the Excelsior Lodge decided to create a sinking fund of $500 to meet future building needs.[17]

In addition to training members in the intricacies of property management, the lodges, which owned more property than was needed to conduct the lodge's functions, often used this resource to advance black enterprise and to meet the black community's needs. For example, the Giblem Lodge in Wilmington was housed in a 3-story building; it used those floors not needed by the lodge for a black cultural center and the city's first library for blacks.[18] Black firms also were housed in the hall. In 1898 the first floor of the lodge was used as a printing office. During the next decade a store and a creamery were located in the same space. In addition to the lodge hall, the Masons of Giblem Lodge rented out the land they owned south of the building to black businessmen. During the 1890s Alfred Hargrave, Wilmington's blacksmith, who had been conducting his trade in the city as a slave since before the war, rented this plot for $3.50 a month to house his shop. The site must have been fairly large, because in 1903 Edward Green, a black undertaker, took out a 5-year lease to rent a building on the land for $5 per month. Evidence of the extent and value of the Giblem Lodge's surplus holdings was the lodge vote of 21 to 3 on 15 January 1903 to sell 35 feet of the tract to one W. Davis for $1,200.

Besides managing their property to the benefit of black entrepreneurs, some lodges had enough funds on reserve to invest. For example, in 1902 the Mount Lebanon Lodge, in Tarboro, purchased 25 shares of stock in the Union Cooperative Investment Company for $50.[19] This firm may have been a black business venture.

Another very visible method by which the Masons financially aided their membership was by dispersing benevolence and charity. Lodges often provided direct short-term financial assistance to those members who faced infirmities or tragedies. In 1908 W. H. Haddock, who had recently lost his crop due to "water damage," received $5 from his fellow members of the Derrick Lodge in Pollocksville.[20] When William Nash, of the Giblem Lodge, became ill in 1898, his fellow lodge members gave him $2 and paid his lodge dues. After Ellis Hayes, who had to provide for himself and his blind wife, became paralyzed in 1908, his fellow members of Rural Hall Lodge, in the village of Rural Hall, gave him $10. That same year the Prince Hall Lodge, in Henderson, generously provided assistance to one member, R. D. Harrison, who needed funds to buy an artificial foot.

Lodges sometimes even aided Masons from other lodges who faced financial problems but could not get immediate aid from their own lodges. For example, in 1875 the Excelsior Lodge in Raleigh received a request for assistance from J. B. Toomer, a Mason from Brunswick, Georgia, who was destitute after attending his father's funeral in Boston. Even though the lodge had very limited funds in its treasury at that time, it loaned him $5. Even if this was not enough money to enable Toomer to get all the way back to Georgia, it may have allowed him to travel far enough to reach a community where another lodge would provide him with support.[21] Although it is impossible to determine exactly how much such assistance aided these lodge members in keeping their land or paying their rent or mortgages, in many cases the support must have been essential or the members would not requested it.

Support of fellow members extended even beyond immediate financial difficulties. In 1899 Anthony Burns, a longtime restaurant owner and member of the Excelsior Lodge in Raleigh, became quite ill. Although the lodge records make no note of it, Burns's fellow lodge members probably spent many hours sitting with him through his illness and providing him with emotional support, a practice so common among the Masons that the lodges formed permanent committees just for that purpose. Despite the comfort of this emotional support and a helpful donation of $5 from the lodge, Burns died in December. His fellow lodge members spent $20 for his coffin and grave and another $3 to rent the carriage for his burial. Again, although there is no record of it, the Excelsior Lodge members very likely practiced the Masonic custom of wearing mourning badges for thirty days following Burns's death.[22]

Masonic financial aid continued even after a member's death. By 1880 the state lodge had created a benevolence plan to provide money to the widows of deceased members. For many years, when a member in the state died every lodge in North Carolina would assess each of its members a quarter to be given to the dead member's widow. As the number of lodges and members grew rapidly during the 1890s, after the turn of the century a more formal, centralized fund was established and managed by the treasurer of the Grand Lodge of North Carolina. In 1908 the Grand Treasurer dispersed $22,925 to widows. During that year the widow's benefit was raised from $175 to $225. By 1910, again marking a large increase in membership in the state, which allowed larger sums to be assessed, the death benefit was raised to $300.[23]

In addition to the state lodge's managing a substantial death benefit, individual lodges felt a long-term commitment to provide assistance to the widows of deceased members. For example, the Giblem Lodge gave widows $3 every year as well as a load of wood during the winter.[24] Support for the families of deceased members also extended to children. The Masons made substantial donations to the state black orphanage in Oxford, North Carolina, which had been created during the 1880s. By

1910 the orphanage, which housed 210 children, was receiving 10 percent of the Grand Lodge of North Carolina's annual revenue. By that
year the Grand Lodge was also giving assistance to another black orphanage in Winston.[25] Moreover, in addition to their general donation, the
Masons may have earmarked support for orphans of deceased lodge
members since contributions were donated for the benefit of specific
children.

Black Masonry in North Carolina clearly provided its members a form
of fellowship that exceeded their immediate social needs. It permitted
black professionals, businessmen, artisans, and farmers, many of whom
had experienced an unusual degree of economic success, to come together and collectively work to improve the condition of the membership and the black community as a whole.

Of all of the collective enterprises engaged in by North Carolina blacks,
the one that received the greatest publicity was the North Carolina
Industrial Association. Not only was it the first statewide organization
formed by economically successful blacks but every year through its
sponsorship of the black state fair it showcased the achievements of this
group.

Under a private incorporation act of the state of North Carolina, the
North Carolina Industrial Association was established on 14 March 1879.
Its founders, 22 black community leaders in Raleigh, outlined the organization's goals: "to encourage and promote the development of the
industrial and educational resources of the colored people of North
Carolina, to gather statistics respecting their progress . . . , to hold
annually . . . an exhibition of the products of their industry and education, and to offer premiums for articles so exhibited." [26]

The most visible effort of the Industrial Association was its sponsorship of the annual black state fair. Beginning in the fall of 1879 and
continuing over forty years, the fair was held each year in Raleigh. During its initial years the fair was supported entirely by private contributions to the Industrial Association, largely from leading white bankers,
businessmen, and industrialists. In 1887, however, the North Carolina
legislature granted $1,000 to fund the enterprise.[27]

A vital factor in the Industrial Association's general success and especially in sponsoring the black fair was the organization's leadership. It was
particularly fortunate to be led by a number of able presidents who represented a wide variety of black professional and business endeavors. For
example, its first president, John S. Leary, was the son of Matthew N.
Leary Jr., one of Fayetteville's leading black harness makers for decades
before the Civil War.[28] After attending Howard University, John Leary

became one of the first blacks to be admitted to the North Carolina bar. In addition to his law practice, Leary served in the North Carolina House, as a federal Internal Revenue collector, as an alderman for Fayetteville, and as a delegate to the Republican Party national convention. Further, he helped create Shaw University's law department and served as its dean. Other prominent presidents of the Industrial Association during its formative years included Dr. Ezekiel E. Smith, of Goldsboro, one of the state's leading black educators as well as the U.S. resident minister and general consul to the Republic of Liberia in 1888, and Warren C. Coleman, of Concord, the founder of the nation's first black-owned and -operated textile mill.[29] During the early twentieth century the organization's presidency was held by Berry O'Kelly, of Raleigh, and John Merrick, of Durham, two of the state's preeminent black businessmen.

In addition to its presidents, the Industrial Association mobilized the efforts of numerous black professionals and business leaders to ensure the success of the annual state black fair. Although the fair lasted for less than a week in early November, the Industrial Association's executive committee spent the preceding nine months making critical arrangements.[30] Since their participation was essential to the success of the fair, usually half of the committee was composed of leading Raleigh businessmen. For example, in 1897 the Raleigh members of the committee, who clearly had much to gain from the influx of thousands of visitors into the capital city, included Charles W. Hoover, a saloon keeper, and Anthony Burns, a leading restaurant owner, among others.[31] In addition to the members of the executive committee from Raleigh, the rest of the membership read virtually like a who's who of the state's black leaders. For example, other members of the 1897 committee included such prominent black politicians as Henry P. Cheatham, of Littleton, the former congressman from North Carolina's Second District; Congressman George White, of Tarboro, who then represented the Second District; and John Holloway, of Wilmington, a former 2-term member of the North Carolina House. Two of its more distinguished black members from the business sector included Richard Fitzgerald, the owner of the major brick-making firm in Durham, and John H. Williamson, of Louisburg, who served as editor of a number of black newspapers in the state.

Foremost among the arrangements made by the executive committee was obtaining the cooperation of railroads in the state.[32] Not only were the railroads essential in providing transportation for those visiting the fair but special arrangements had to be made with them to transport the various articles and exhibits that attracted people to the event. The Industrial Association was able not only to obtain free passes from many railroads to aid the organization's leaders in their various activities but also to convince the lines to provide reduced prices for tickets for those attending the fair.

The executive committee appears to have used its extensive state black business network to advertise the fair as well as to attract exhibiters. One factor that particularly aided the Industrial Association's efforts and may have been an outgrowth of the success of the state black fair was the rise of local black fairs. By 1885 a series of black fairs was being held in nine North Carolina towns and villages during the early fall. Members of the executive committee spoke at these fairs to encourage blacks to attend the upcoming black state fair a few weeks later. For example, in 1885 John H. Williamson, the secretary of the Industrial Association, spoke to local black fairs in Chapel Hill and Mebanesville. Likewise, a number of the members of the executive committee attended the black fair in Durham in October 1896.[33] By the 1890s the fair in New Bern had become such a major event in the eastern part of the state that in 1895 the community's black political and business leaders formally incorporated their organization as the Oriental, Industrial Stock, Fruit, and Agricultural Fair Association.[34] Leaders of the Industrial Association especially were sure to attend this event, held annually in late August, to make the contacts necessary for promoting the later event in Raleigh.[35]

Once the state black fair convened in Raleigh, one of the major activities was the judging of events. Now the role of black businessmen and prominent farmers who belonged to the Industrial Association became paramount, as they served as judges of these exhibits. Most exhibitors, especially those in such household crafts as quilt making, had little to gain from the recognition they might receive at the fair outside of personal satisfaction and small financial prizes. However, awards that signified quality of livestock production and particular skilled crafts might make a substantial difference in one's business prospects. For example, as early as the first fair, in 1879, an award was given for the best saddlery and harness exhibit. Significantly, Lemuel B. Hinton, one of Raleigh's well-known craftsmen in this trade, served as judge in this area.[36]

As important as the state black fair was as an organizational activity and showcase for the state's leading black businessmen and farmers, for most in attendance the event was a social activity. Prominent visitors to the fair were even listed in the black newspaper.[37] In fact, since so many of the state's black leaders congregated in Raleigh to attend the fair, they often used this opportunity to hold important political, business, and social gatherings. For example, during the 1891 fair a black political con-

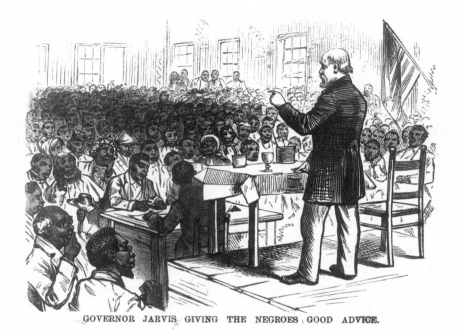

GOVERNOR JARVIS GIVING THE NEGROES GOOD ADVICE.

8. North Carolina Governor Thomas J. Jarvis addressing the first black state fair, Raleigh, 1879. Jarvis told the assembly of blacks, "You must have classes among yourselves. White people have them." (Courtesy of North Carolina Division of Archives and History, N76.9.67A)

vention was held, a meeting took place on the prospects of creating a black bank in the state, and the black Hesperian Literary and Social Club assembled.[38]

A final important event of the black state fair was the speeches presented by major black and white leaders. If any speech symbolizes the nature of the Industrial Association and its black fair, it is the one given by Governor Thomas J. Jarvis on the opening day of the first fair, in 1879. Governor Jarvis told the assembly of blacks who had been brought together by some of the most successful leaders of their race in the state, "You must have classes among yourselves. White people have them." According to the governor, blacks of the better class were "those who are trying to accumulate property."[39] The governor's words must have held special meaning for the members of the Industrial Association, who for many years would use their organization to associate with other blacks who had experienced economic success and to work to promote the opportunities for others of their race.

As soon as blacks gained the franchise and elected members of their race to the state legislature, they began to create financial institutions to aid them in their effort to gain land and conduct businesses. In 1869, during the first state legislature that contained black members, bills were introduced to incorporate black-owned land and building associations in two North Carolina cities, Fayetteville and New Bern, and four counties, Wake, Warren, Halifax, and Guilford. The next year two additional institutions were chartered.[40]

These land and building associations were structured along similar lines. All had a projected capital stock ranging from $100,000 to $500,000, which was divided into shares ranging from $10 to $200. The institution usually would not begin to function until the first 100 shares were purchased. As for their planned activities, the Fayetteville Co-operative Land and Building Association's were quite typical, as the entity received the power to buy, sell, lease, and mortgage property.

The leadership of these new financial institutions was composed of men who were among the most prominent black economic and political leaders in their communities. In fact, nine black legislators sat on the various incorporation boards of the initial six institutions.[41] For example, among the 12 men who incorporated the Warren County Co-operative Business Company were William Cawthorne and Richard Faulkner, members of the state house, and John A. Hyman, a state senator.[42] In addition, Albert Burgess and Henry H. Plummer, members of the Warren County board of assessors, served as incorporators. These five were joined by the diversified entrepreneur William S. Williams, described earlier, and John Batchelor, the merchant who conducted a grocery store in Warrenton from 1868 to 1872. Likewise, among the incorporators of the Fayetteville Co-operative Land and Building Association were Matthew N. Leary Jr., the antebellum free mulatto saddler who owned real estate valued at $5,000 in 1870, his son John, a member of the legislature and one of the state's leading black attorneys, and many other black landowners.[43]

The effectiveness of these six initial black financial institutions and the three incorporated during the next legislative session in assisting blacks to gain land and run businesses is unclear. Since no mention of them was made after their incorporation, some, if not most, may have failed to acquire the required number of shareholders and therefore never actually functioned. The early and mid 1870s were especially difficult years to find investors in such ventures for two reasons. First, the business panic that began in 1873 and lasted for a number of years clearly was not a climate conducive for building and loan associations. Second, many blacks had placed their savings in the Freedmen's Savings and Trust Company, which had been chartered in 1865. The records of

the three branches of this bank in Raleigh, New Bern, and Wilmington
indicate that thousands of North Carolina blacks, many of whom lived
quite some distance from these cities, had deposited money in the
bank.[44] The national financial crisis of 1873 led to the failure of the
Freedmen's bank in 1874, and the bank's inability to compensate its de-
positors discouraged many blacks from placing their money in any financial institution, even those whose aim was to advance their race.[45]

In addition to the poor economic conditions that prevailed through
the 1870s nationwide and then again during the latter 1880s in North
Carolina, politics also may have played a role in preventing other black
financial institutions from forming. When black political strength was at
its nadir, after the end of Reconstruction and throughout the 1880s, it
may have been difficult for blacks who sought to create a financial institution with limited liability to get the legislature to pass such incorporation bills. Significantly, during the early 1890s, when black political
power was again on the ascendancy in North Carolina, there was another
flourish of activity in collective black financial endeavors. By 1891 the
black-operated Eastern Building and Loan Association was operating in
the state.[46] That same year another building and loan association, cen-
tered in Wilmington, held $60,000 in stock. The latter establishment was
so prosperous that there was talk that it soon might become "a full-
fledged banking institution." [47] However, these institutions, like their
predecessors twenty years before, must have run into difficulty when the
national economy fell into a depression during the early and mid 1890s.
The Eastern Building and Loan Association faltered in 1893, the year
the national business panic began. As a sign of the firm's collapse,
Isaac H. Smith, the prominent black New Bern financier, sued the institution for $46,000 that year. In addition to the problems Smith had with
the firm, one publication noted, "A great many persons have lost money
in this association whether through their own or the institution's fault,
we are not prepared to say." [48]

Although there was substantial interest in creating a black bank in the
state during the early 1890s, the national financial crisis prevented any
progress in advancing that effort.[49] By 1897, with the financial climate
improved and black political power at its highest point since Reconstruction, there was a renewed attempt to create such an institution. In fact,
that year two black banks were established. The first to be formed, the
Mutual Aid Banking Company of New Bern, was incorporated by the
state legislature in March. Except for the names of the eight men who
served as its board of incorporation, all of whom were leading businessmen of the city, nothing is known about the institution except that it
opened its doors on 15 August.[50]

More is known about the second black bank, the Dime Bank of Kinston, which was formed later than the Mutual Aid Banking Company but actually began operations a month earlier, on 1 July 1897. Charles F. Dunn, one of Kinston's most affluent black storekeepers for nearly two decades, owned the Dime Bank. An advertisement for the bank noted that it was a member of the American Bankers' Association. The bank would receive deposits from individuals and corporations for "any sum not less than 10 cents" and would pay 6 percent per annum interest on all deposits of more than $5 that remained in the bank for at least 30 days. Further, it would process accounts through the mail. In order to build confidence in the firm, it was stressed that the funds would be stored in "one of the latest Mosier, Bahman & Co" fireproof safes, which had been made to order for the bank.[51]

There are no records about the level of success these two banks experienced. Ten years after they opened they were not even noted in a significant study conducted that year of black banks in the nation.[52] In 1907 the only black bank in North Carolina that was mentioned by that study was the Forsyth Savings and Trust Company of Winston-Salem, which had just been established by Simon G. Atkins, the president of the Slater Normal and Industrial School for blacks and later president of Winston-Salem College. By the beginning of 1909 this bank had about $13,000 in deposits and was doing a weekly business of about $5,000. It had more than $15,000 in total resources, and it had transacted more than $275,000 in business since its inception. The bank remained in business until the outset of the Depression, when it, like most other black banks in the nation, failed.[53]

The same year the Forsyth Savings and Trust Company was created, the Mechanics and Farmers Bank of Durham was incorporated by the state legislature.[54] The Mechanics and Farmers Bank was formed with an initial capital stock of $10,000, with stock shares valued at $25. The Mechanics and Farmers Bank was closely tied to the North Carolina Mutual and Provident Association, the black-owned insurance company incorporated in 1899, whose name would be changed to the North Carolina Mutual Life Insurance Company in 1919.[55] Not only would the two institutions share the same building for many years but four of the five men who served as incorporators of the insurance company, John Merrick, Dr. Aaron McDuffie Moore, James E. Shepherd, and William G. Pearson, later created the bank. John Merrick, who was born a slave in 1859, worked as a brickmason after the war. After selecting barbering as a new trade, Merrick emerged as one of the leading black barbers in the state and by 1892 owned a number of barbershops in Durham, where he had taken up residence 12 years earlier.[56] By 1910 he was the largest black landowner in that city and collected an estimated $550 in rents monthly from his property.[57]

Merrick's leading partner, Aaron McDuffie Moore, the son of a wealthy antebellum mulatto farmer in Columbus County, received a medical degree from Leonard Medical School of Shaw University in 1888.[58] After choosing Durham as the community in which to begin his practice, he established the Durham Drug Company along with Richard Fitzgerald, Durham's prominent brick manufacturer, James E. Shepherd and Jesse A. Dodson, two graduates of the School of Pharmacy of Shaw University, and William G. Pearson, a public-school principal. Fitzgerald and Dodson later participated in creating the bank.

Besides their common financial interests, these men shared other important ties. Merrick, Fitzgerald, Pearson, and Stanford L. Warren, another founder of the bank, all were active members of, and donors to, Durham's St. Joseph African Methodist Episcopal Church. A number of the other leaders of the North Carolina Mutual Life Insurance Company and the Mechanics and Farmers Bank were members of the community's other prominent black church, the White Rock Baptist. And four of the incorporators of the bank were members of Durham's Doric Masonic Lodge.[59]

When the Mechanics and Farmers Bank opened in August 1908, Fitzgerald served as president, Merrick as vice-president, and Pearson as cashier. By 1920 the bank had increased its capital stock from the initial offering of $10,000 to $49,335. That year, with just over $300,000 in total resources, the bank possessed a bit more than half of all the financial resources of black banks in the state. Its status as the preeminent black financial institution in North Carolina would only be enhanced when it became the sole such institution to survive the Depression.[60]

The strength of the Mechanics and Farmers Bank can be attributed to the close ties it maintained to the leading black businessmen of Durham and especially to the North Carolina Mutual Life Insurance Company. All 12 of the members of the board of directors in 1920 were residents of Durham. Four of the directors, Jesse A. Dodson, Stanford L. Warren, Aaron Moore, and William G. Pearson, had served as original incorporators of the bank 12 years earlier. They were now joined on the board by John Merrick's son, Edward, who had run the North Carolina Mutual's Georgia branch, and Aaron Moore's nephew, Charles Clinton Spaulding, who had been instrumental in managing the insurance company and had served on its board of directors since its second year. In fact, as further evidence of the continuing link between the two major black institutions, in addition to Spaulding, fellow directors of both establishments included Pearson, Merrick, and John M. Avery.[61] The other members of the bank's board were equally distinguished black residents of Durham: J. C. Scarborough, Durham's affluent undertaker; P. H. Smith, a leading merchant; W. J. Jordan, a realtor; J. A. Dyer, an auditor; and J. H. Dunston, a minister.

In addition to their local and statewide collective efforts, North Carolina blacks promoted enterprise by participating in national business organizations, foremost among them the National Negro Business League, organized by Booker T. Washington in 1900. Although there are no records specifying when North Carolina blacks first joined the League, John Merrick and Aaron Moore, of Durham, did represent the North Carolina Mutual at the organization's founding convention. The first recorded speech by a North Carolinian at a League annual convention occurred in 1902, when Jesse A. Dodson, the Durham drugstore proprietor who six years later would participate in the incorporation of the Mechanics and Farmers Bank, addressed the League on his firm's success.[62] Shortly thereafter, blacks in New Bern received the state's first League charter, the 94th charter granted by the League in the country. By the time the League convened its ninth annual convention in Baltimore in 1908, New Bern had been joined by chapters in six other North Carolina communities: Wilmington, Greensboro, Charlotte, Wilson, Asheville, and Statesville. The next year a state organization was created.[63]

Unlike the black fraternal orders, which after the turn of the century began to extend their membership to residents of some of North Carolina's smallest hamlets and rural crossroads, by 1916 the League had chapters in only 24 communities, most of which were large. Only two communities with fewer than 1,000 residents had received charters, and the median population of communities with chapters was 6,500.[64]

The League's confinement to the larger communities of North Carolina is also reflected by the type of black business communities that had chapters. All 24 of the communities that had received chapters by 1915 contained at least one credit-rated black firm. Although they represented only one-fifth of the communities that contained black credit-rated firms, these 24 communities included nearly half of such firms.[65]

The problems encountered in trying to organize a chapter in a small community are illustrated by the case of Walter P. Evans, of Laurinburg, North Carolina, who wrote the National Negro Business League in 1914 requesting help in creating a chapter in his community.[66] For at least 25 years Evans had operated a general store in the town, which had nearly doubled in population since 1900 but still had only 2,500 residents. "I am the only merchant here," Evans declared. "It's necessary for me to rely on the farmers, mechanics, barbers & doctors &c to effect

the organization now to make it fruitful." Evans submitted the names
of 13 individuals, including 5 farmers, 3 artisans, 1 minister, 1 doctor,
1 insurance agent, 1 barber, and 1 hotel manager. He asked the national
organization to write these men and encourage them to join. Evidently
his efforts failed, because Laurinburg did not receive a chapter.

Communities such as Laurinburg may have failed to create a chapter
partly because of the cost of membership. Although the $2 League mem-
bership dues may not have been especially prohibitive, it would have
been difficult to find enough men in a small community who could pay
this fee in order to receive a charter.[67] Prospective members like those
included on Walter Evans's list for Laurinburg, probably faced the problem of paying similar dues for membership in other organizations. For
example, Evans himself was already the secretary of his local Masonic
lodge, and at least four of the men on his list belonged to nearby lodges
of that fraternal order.[68]

Another reason why the National Negro Business League tended to
be focused in larger communities may have been the organization's emphasis on the success of substantial black entrepreneurs. Through the
publication *Notes on Racial Progress,* as well as in speeches at the national
convention, the League continually stressed the most notable achievements of black businessmen. For example, in 1910 *Notes on Racial Progress*
described a textile mill owned and operated by blacks that would soon
be opening in Durham.[69] The mill had been incorporated with $50,000.
The men who stood "largely behind this business venture," John Merrick and Richard Fitzgerald, were "reputed to be the richest Negroes in
North Carolina." Merrick's emergence as one of North Carolina's leading black businessmen has already been described. The rise of his partner in the textile-mill venture was equally impressive. Richard Fitzgerald
was the son of a free Maryland black father and a white mother; the
family had moved from Pennsylvania to the Durham area a few years
after the war.[70] After only a few years the Fitzgeralds had created one of
the largest brick-manufacturing firms in the state, producing 30,000
bricks a day by 1910. Richard Fitzgerald owned $50,000 worth of real
estate. His grandniece described his home as "a fine 18-room slate-
roofed house of many turrets and gables and a wide piazza, set in a large
maple and magnolia grove and surrounded by white sandy drives and
terraced lawns."

The League tended to use its annual national convention to highlight
the achievements of men like Merrick and Fitzgerald, who clearly stood
at the apex of black entrepreneurship in North Carolina. At the same
League convention in Boston where Berry O'Kelly described his remarkable success, Charles C. Spaulding, one of the leaders of the North Caro-

lina Mutual Life Insurance Company, spoke about his firm.[71] He noted that North Carolina Mutual did $404,766 business annually, operated in three states, and employed 700 workers.

Although all black businessmen could appreciate such stories, it probably was somewhat difficult for many of them, especially for craftsmen and those engaged in small firms, to feel a close bond with men whose achievements seemed so stellar. Further, for most black businessmen membership in the League offered few prospects for advancing their opportunities. Although the leading businessmen may have gained from the contacts they made through their involvement in the League's many subsidiary societies, for the typical black firm, whose clientele resided in their community, the advantages of local reputation, which could be attained by membership in fraternal orders like Masonry, far outweighed national connections.[72] Hence, although the National Negro Business League played an important role in bringing economically successful black North Carolinians together and introducing them to blacks throughout the nation with whom they shared some experiences, for most North Carolina blacks the organization was of only limited value.

Given the difficult economic and social circumstances that the vast majority of North Carolina blacks faced after 1865, many blacks likely believed that the surest path to success was through the pursuit of their individual well-being. If the history of enterprising blacks during the 50 years following the Civil War was characterized largely by the achievements of individuals, the positive impact of collective efforts toward enterprise encouraging the improvement of the race at the same time that they promoted individual success is equally visible.

The Politics of Enterprise

IN 1860 Henry C. Cherry, a 24-year-old free mulatto carpenter residing in Edgecombe County, owned no property.[1] By 1870 he owned real estate valued at $1,000 and had already served as a delegate to the North Carolina Constitutional Convention in 1868 and one term in the state assembly. In addition to maintaining his carpentry firm, during the 1880s Cherry ran a combination grocery and liquor establishment in Tarboro. Although he was elected to the state legislature for only a single term, Cherry also served on the county commission of Edgecombe. Further, Cherry maintained ties to politics through his three sons-in-law. His daughter Louise had married Henry P. Cheatham, and his daughter Cora had married George H. White, two of the most influential black officeholders in North Carolina during the 1880s and 1890s. These rivals were elected to the U.S. House of Representatives to represent North Carolina's Second Congressional District for a total of four terms. Further, another of Cherry's daughters, Georgie, was the wife of Eustace E. Green, a member of the state assembly from Wilmington.

To what degree their own involvement in politics and the political participation of their relatives allowed black landowners and businessmen like Henry Cherry to advance their individual and collective racial economic standing was revealed in a 1906 editorial in one of the leading publications of black North Carolinians. This editorial, which appeared in the *Quarterly Review* of the African Methodist Episcopal Zion Church a few years after most North Carolina blacks ceased being allowed to vote, observed, "All we have and are, came through politics, and it is too late in the day to try to curry favor with somebody by declaring the opposite of a recognized truth."[2]

The obvious starting point for observing the role enterprising black North Carolinians played in politics is the state constitutional convention of 1868, the first statewide governmental body to which blacks were elected. The 13 blacks who were elected as delegates to this convention, which shaped the new structure of state and local government, included some of the leading black politicians of Reconstruction.[3] Ten of the 13 delegates later would be elected to the state senate or the state assembly. One delegate, John H. Hyman, of Warren County, would serve in the United States House of Representatives.

In addition to their service in government, a number of the black delegates to the 1868 constitutional convention were prominent landowners and businessmen. Having been free before the war, many of these men found themselves in the favorable economic position after the war described in chapters 1 and 2, above. For example, like the aforementioned Henry Cherry, Parker Robbins, a delegate from Bertie County, was a free mulatto mechanic in 1860. That year he owned $250 in real estate as well as $415 in personal estate. After paying his county taxes in 1862 and appearing on the Confederate tax census for that year, Parker, along with his younger brother Augustus, enlisted in the 2nd U.S. Colored Cavalry. Parker held the rank of sergeant-major, and Augustus served on the field staff.[4] After returning to Bertie after the war, Parker owned a farm worth $500. In addition to serving as a delegate to the constitutional convention, Parker represented Bertie County for two terms in the state assembly. His brother Augustus also later represented Bertie in the state assembly while running a liquor store in Windsor, the county seat of Bertie.

Cuffie Mayo, of Granville County, another black delegate to the 1868 constitutional convention, had been a 57-year-old free black painter in 1860. Although he owned no real estate before the war, he held $50 in personal estate. Two years after Cuffie served in the constitutional convention, he completed his sole term in the state assembly and owned $600 in real estate and $200 in personal estate.

Wilson Cary, of Caswell County, was another black delegate who had been free before the war. A native of Amelia County, Virginia, Cary had moved to Caswell County in 1855. By 1870 he had accumulated $800 in real estate. In addition to farming, he also taught. Cary was the only black delegate to the 1868 convention who also served as a delegate to the 1875 state constitutional convention. Besides holding a number of county offices, Cary represented Caswell for five noncontinuous terms in the state assembly from 1868, when he was first elected, until 1889.

Another delegate to the 1868 convention who had been free before the war, John Hyman, had served as a janitor for a northern-born businessman in Warrenton during the late 1850s.[5] Hyman seems to have spent most of the war in Alabama and did not return to North Carolina until 1865. After returning to Warrenton, he opened a combination general store and liquor establishment in 1868. That same year he moved into politics by serving as a delegate to the 1868 convention; after that he was elected to two consecutive terms as a state senator. His business career also seems to have fared quite well, for by 1870 he owned $3,500 in property. However, his involvement in politics may have engaged too much of Hyman's energy, because by 1872 his mercantile firm closed. This was only a minor setback for Hyman, for two years later he was elected to the U.S. House of Representatives.

One of North Carolina's wealthiest black landowners, James H. Harris, of Wake County, also was a delegate to the 1868 convention.[6] Harris, the owner of $5,000 in property in 1870, was born in Granville County in about 1830. After being apprenticed to an Englishman in Warren County, who taught Harris the mattress-making and upholstering trade, at age 19 he started his own business in Raleigh. In 1856 he left North Carolina and moved to Oberlin, Ohio, where he attended college for two years. During the early years of the Civil War he traveled extensively in Canada, Liberia, and Sierra Leone. In 1863 he was commissioned by Governor Levi Morton of Indiana to raise a regiment of black soldiers. Soon after the war he returned to North Carolina as a teacher for the New England Freedmen's Aid Society. He quickly became involved in organizing blacks politically and was a charter member of the Republican Party in the state. In addition to being a delegate in the 1868 convention, he served a number of terms in the state assembly and the state senate and was also a Raleigh city alderman. His interest in politics was not confined to North Carolina, as he also attended the 1868, 1872, and 1876 Republican national convention.

Abraham Galloway was another black delegate to the 1868 constitutional convention who had left his native state during his youth, but under very different circumstances than those of James Harris.[7] Galloway's mother was a slave, and his white father was a member of the wealthy Galloway family of the Cape Fear region. After spending his early years as one of his father's slaves, Abraham escaped in 1857 and fled to Ohio. He returned to North Carolina during the war as a spy for the Union army. During the war he also served as a delegate to the National Convention of Colored Citizens of the United States, which created the National Equal Rights League. After the war Galloway returned to North Carolina as an agent for the National Equal Rights League. Although he was a landowning farmer in Brunswick County, Galloway was elected as a delegate from neighboring New Hanover County to the 1868 convention. After being elected twice to the state senate as well as being selected as a presidential elector, Galloway's career was cut short in 1870 by his premature death from disease.

The pattern black landowners and businessmen initially set for participation in the 1868 constitutional convention carried over into service in the state legislature during the Reconstruction period. In addition to those delegates already mentioned who owned land or conducted firms, many other affluent blacks were elected to the state assembly or the state senate. In fact, more than half of the 19 blacks elected to the legislature before 1870 (52.6 percent) were landowners. Hence, black members of the legislature were nearly eight times more likely to own real estate than other members of their race. Significantly, during these early years African-American legislators, like businessmen, were disproportionately mulattoes. This pattern continued throughout the 1870s. Two-fifths of the 70 who were elected to the legislature between 1868 and 1878 owned real estate—about six times the state average—and of those whose color can be determined, nearly three-fifths were mulattoes.[8]

Reflective of their skin color, a number of the members of the state legislature during the late 1860s and early 1870s had been antebellum freedmen. Israel B. Abbott, a member of the state assembly from Craven County, had been a free mulatto in 1860. In 1870, two years before he was elected to the assembly, Abbott, a house carpenter, owned $300 in real estate and $400 in personal estate. In 1880 and 1884 Abbott attended the Republican national convention.

Hawkins H. Carter, a mulatto who represented Warren County in the state assembly for three terms during the 1870s and who later served two terms in the state senate during the early 1880s, had owned a farm worth $175 in 1860. Five years after the war ended his farm had increased in value to $300.

Although he owned no land in his own name when he was elected to the state assembly from Cumberland County in 1868, John S. Leary was the son of one of the wealthiest mulatto families in the state both before and after the war.[9] Matthew Leary, John's father, conducted a saddlery and harness-making firm of such prominence that it was credit-rated as early as 1848. Two years after John was elected to the legislature his father owned property worth $6,000.

Other landowning mulattoes who apparently were slaves before the war also were elected to the legislature during Reconstruction. For example, John R. Page, a mulatto house carpenter who in 1870 was elected by the voters of Chowan County to the state assembly, owned $420 in real estate and $300 in personal estate. Apparently the 1870s would prove to be quite a prosperous decade for Page, for by the end of that decade he was described by a credit rater as the owner of two farms, one of which was located in neighboring Bertie County, in addition to being the operator of a fish store.[10]

Hugh Cale, a grocer in Elizabeth City, in Pasquotank County, who was elected to the state assembly for the first of four terms in 1876, was another mulatto who apparently had not been free before the war. In 1870 Cale owned $1,300 in property. Cale's estate continued to grow after he became a legislator; by 1885 he owned farmland, seven city lots, and personal property valued at $2,750.[11]

Although they had not enjoyed the advantage of antebellum freedom, a number of legislators during these years who were enumerated as being black also accumulated considerable wealth and prominence in business. Richard Tucker, a black undertaker in Craven County, owned $1,000 in real estate and $500 in personal property in 1870, the year he was elected to the state assembly. Likewise, Hanson T. Hughes, a black barber from Granville County who served two terms in the state assembly and one term in the state senate during the 1870s, owned $1,000 in land and $250 in personal property in 1870, despite no evidence of having been free before the war.

Although black political opportunities in North Carolina were diminished by the conclusion of Reconstruction, they did not disappear entirely. Moreover, although the backgrounds of the blacks who served in the state legislature shifted somewhat, there was considerable continuity. This continuity resulted from a number of factors, the most notable being that nearly one-fourth of the blacks who served in the legislature before 1880 were elected to that body at least once again during the 1880s and 1890s.[12] A number of those legislators who served in both eras, such as Hugh Cale, Hawkins Carter, Wilson Cary, and James Harris, have already been described. Two of the other 11 men who fit this pattern and who were particularly prominent were William Henry Crews and John Hendrick Williamson.

William Henry Crews represented Granville County in the state assembly for a total of five terms, two terms during the 1870s and three during the 1890s. Born a slave in 1844, Crews was taken from his mother and raised by a white woman. Indeed, indicative of his unusual upbring-

ing, Crews, who was reportedly unaware that slavery existed until he was
12, was allowed to attend the public and private schools of Oxford. In
addition to being elected to the state assembly for five terms, Crews held
a number of offices in Granville County and in his hometown of Oxford,
including those of sheriff, constable, ranger, school committee member,
and street commissioner. Further, he served for 16 years as treasurer and
for 22 years as deacon of the First Baptist Church of Oxford. He earned
his living by farming and teaching.

John Hendrick Williamson, who represented Franklin County during
five terms during the 1860s, 1870s, and 1880s, was born a slave in Cov-
ington, Georgia, in 1844.[13] Upon the death of his master in the late
1850s John and his parents were moved by the deceased slaveholder's
widow to Louisburg, in Franklin County, North Carolina, where John was
hired out as a slave. As early as 1867 he was appointed a registrar of
voters in Franklin County by General Daniel E. Sickles, the commander
of the Second Military District, which included North and South Carolina. In addition to being elected to the 1868 state constitutional convention and the state assembly on five occasions, Williamson was defeated in
three other campaigns for the legislature. Besides holding a number of
county offices, he was a delegate to the Republican national convention
in 1872, 1884, and 1888. During the 1880s and 1890s he edited a number of newspapers, most notably the *Raleigh Gazette,* the leading nonsec-
tarian black publication in the state. A further indication of his strong
ties with North Carolina's black business community is that for a number of years he served as secretary of the North Carolina Industrial
Association.

The black members of the legislature who served terms before and
after 1880 generally had been born during the 1830s and 1840s and had
spent many years as slaves before their election to the legislature.[14]
Therefore, despite their considerable accomplishments after emancipation, their enslavement during the formative years of their lives clearly
restricted their achievements.

In contrast to these early legislators, about two-thirds of the blacks
elected to the legislature for the first time during the 1880s and 1890s
had been born after 1850; a few of them had been born after the war.[15]
The most visible advantage of being emancipated while still in their
youth was their enhanced opportunity to attend school and to enter professions that had always been closed to members of their race. Most of
these black legislators appear to have received the equivalent of a modern high-school education, and more than one-third of them actually
attended college.[16] Most of those who attended college were enrolled at

Shaw University in Raleigh, a black institution sponsored by the Baptist Church, but others matriculated at the other major black institutions of this era, including Biddle College in Charlotte, North Carolina, Hampton Institute in Hampton, Virginia, Howard University in Washington D.C., and Lincoln University in rural southeastern Pennsylvania.

Most of these college-educated legislators had established careers as educators or lawyers before they entered politics and were elected to the state assembly or senate. George H. White, one of Henry C. Cherry's sons-in-law, combined both professions.[17] After graduating from Howard University in 1877, White served as principal of the black grade school, the Presbyterian parochial school, and the state normal school in New Bern. While serving as an educator he also studied law under Judge William J. Clarke and received his law license in 1879. One year later he was elected to represent Craven County in the state assembly.

Henry Cherry's other two sons-in-law, Henry P. Cheatham and Eustace E. Green, also received college degrees and taught before entering politics. Henry Cheatham graduated from Shaw University in 1883 and served as a principal of the black normal school in Plymouth before being elected to his initial office, the registrar of deeds of Vance County.[18] Although he never ran for either the state assembly or the state senate, Cheatham did study law, though he never became a practicing attorney. Eustace E. Green, a graduate of Lincoln University, served as a county examiner of public schools and a principal of a grade school before being elected to serve New Hanover in the state assembly for one term during the early 1880s.

Henry Cherry's sons-in-law were not the only politicians who began their careers in education. Another legislator of this era who very briefly combined employment in education with a career in law was James Eaton, a state assemblyman from Vance County in the late 1890s. Having had the fortune of being born to "thrifty and enterprising" parents who had acquired 700 acres in Franklin County, Eaton was able to attend Shaw University as an undergraduate and later to graduate from its law department.[19] Eaton worked in education for only a very short time, when he managed the black public schools of Henderson from 1897 to 1898. Besides practicing law, he was appointed one of the few black notary publics in North Carolina and also was selected as county attorney of Vance County by the county commissioners.

Some of the black legislators who were attorneys never served as educators. For example, Robert W. Williamson, who represented Caswell County in the state assembly in 1893, graduated from Biddle University in 1890. After studying law under Judge W. H. Bailey, he was admitted to the bar in September 1890. He began his practice in the town of Milton in his home county, then opened an office in New Bern after marrying Georgia Davis, a resident of that city.

In addition to the post-1880 black legislators fortunate enough to get an education that opened up career doors for them before they entered politics, many black members of the state assembly and house were elevated to their offices after taking advantage of the political patronage system. Although patronage positions had been available to blacks during Reconstruction, generally these posts were dispersed upon the recommendation of members of the state assembly and the senate. By the 1880s and 1890s blacks were using the patronage system as a stepping stone to the legislature.

For example, when James H. Young represented Wake County in the state assembly for two terms during the 1890s he already had established a career in patronage positions.[20] In 1858 Young was born in Henderson to a slave mother and, very importantly, a prominent white father who provided for his son's education and career. After attending the common schools of Henderson as well as Shaw University, in 1877 he was given a post in the Internal Revenue Office of the Fourth District of North Carolina by a Colonel J. J. Young, who may have been his father. Although his family connection may have led to his initial appointment, by 1882 Young's demonstrated skills allowed him to attain the rank of chief clerk and cashier in the Fourth District Revenue Office, for which he was paid $1,200 a year.[21] Even the election of a Democratic administration could not keep Young out of patronage positions. After being replaced by a white Democrat in the revenue office during President Grover Cleveland's first term, he was able to use his friends' influence in local government to become the chief clerk in the office of the registrar of deeds in Wake County.

With the election of a Republican administration in 1888, Young reentered the federal patronage system, receiving an appointment as special inspector of customs. Shortly thereafter, President Benjamin Harrison gave him one of the major federal patronage plums in the state, collector of customs for the port of Wilmington. However, North Carolina's Democratic leadership blocked his appointment by encouraging their allies in the U.S. Senate to deny confirmation. Shut out from any position during President Cleveland's second term, Young served for five years as editor of the *Raleigh Gazette*. During this period he was one of the major architects of fusion between the Republican and Populist Parties, an alliance that dislodged the Democrats from power in North Carolina during the mid 1890s. It was during this period that he was elected to represent Wake County for two terms in the state assembly. By this time he was the owner of nine lots in Raleigh valued at $6,600, and he had married the daughter of Stewart Ellison, one of the major black members of the legislature during Reconstruction and a prominent Raleigh businessman.

At the height of his political career Young received a patronage position from the white Republican governor, Daniel Russell, and with the outbreak of the Spanish-American War he was appointed colonel of a regiment of black volunteers designated as the 3rd North Carolina Infantry. Although Young's fall from power came rapidly when the Democrats regained control of the state legislature during the late 1890s, he was able to obtain from President William McKinley an appointment as deputy revenue collector for the Raleigh district, a position he retained under Presidents Theodore Roosevelt and William Howard Taft.

Another example of a black legislator of the 1880s and 1890s who held a patronage position before being elected to the legislature is John T. Howe, who represented New Hanover County in the state assembly for a single term during the late 1890s.[22] Howe had the advantage of being the son of an antebellum freedman, Alfred Howe, a house carpenter who owned $3,000 in property in 1870. In addition, Alfred Howe held a major patronage post as a director of the Freedmen's Savings Bank in Wilmington and served as an alderman on the city council and a member of the county commission of New Hanover during the late 1860s and early 1870s. In 1876 he waged an unsuccessful campaign to gain the Republican nomination for lieutenant governor.[23] The Howe family clearly wielded political power in Wilmington; by the mid 1880s John had received the lucrative patronage appointment of mail carrier in the community, which brought an annual salary of $850.[24] However, there were limits even to the Howes' influence. In 1897, when John attempted to gain the post of collector of customs in Wilmington, which carried an annual salary of $4,000, he was defeated by John C. Dancy Jr., who had held this position until 1894, when he was removed by the Democrats under President Cleveland.[25] The Dancys always matched, and sometimes surpassed, the Howes in black political influence.

Not all the black legislators during the final two decades of the nineteenth century who had held patronage positions before being elected to the legislature had been as prominent as James Young or had had the advantage of antebellum freedom and being a member of a prominent black family like John Howe. E. H. Sutton, a state assemblyman elected from Chowan County in 1882, was born a slave in Perquimans County in 1849. After being educated in Charlotte and Edenton, but evidently not attending college, Sutton was given a position in the Government Printing Office in Washington D.C.

Although many post-1880 black legislators had the advantage of a college education, a profession in education or law, or a patronage post, the most common route to membership in the state assembly or senate was through a career in business. In the legislature black businessmen outnumbered those with other occupations, particularly farmers, because although most North Carolina blacks lived in rural communities, they tended to elect members of their race who were residents of the villages, towns, and cities of their assembly or senate districts. Their urban residence allowed black businessmen the concentrated nucleus of supporters necessary for gaining the Republican Party's nomination. The position of an educator was also a very visible and respected one in urban areas. Black ministers also had a similar status, but the diverse denominational composition of black voters in an entire assembly or senate district seems to have prevented many clergymen from gaining the Republican nomination.[26]

Black businessmen were in a particularly favorable position to be elected to the legislature for a number of reasons. Like urban educators, they held a very visible position in their towns and cities. However, even more than teachers and education administrators, black businessmen were financially secure enough to leave their trades to clerks or assistants for the weeks when they attended the legislature. And since they probably were extending credit to many of their constituents, there was a natural feeling of obligation between black voters and black businessmen.

An example of a black businessman from this period who clearly would have had an extensive knowledge of his constituents was John E. Hussey, Craven County's assemblyman for three terms during the mid and late 1880s. Although he was born a slave in Duplin County in 1849, Hussey was described in 1887 as an individual with the "spirit of true manhood" who "went to work to repair the mental slavery that he had before endured" and emerged as a "self-made man" who now stood "well among his people." As early as 1880 Hussey was running a credit-rated general store in New Bern. During the 1890s he also opened one of the few black-managed boarding houses in the state; this firm remained opened as late as 1915.

The business career of one of Hussey's fellow black members of the state assembly in 1887, Charles Wesley Hoover, again demonstrates the advantage businessmen had when they ran for the legislature. Born a slave in Asheboro in 1854, Hoover had moved to Raleigh in 1869. As early as 1875 he was conducting a credit-rated general store in the state capital. During the 1880s he also began selling liquor. By the turn of the century he had opened what was probably the first black-operated department store in North Carolina. During his only term of service in the state assembly, which he achieved after six years as an alderman in Raleigh, Hoover was termed a "successful businessman" who "made many friends and few enemies in his intercourse with the people."[27]

In addition to serving as important symbols for their race, the black state assemblymen and senators from 1868 to the end of the century were able to help their race by means of their power to introduce private bills in the state legislature. The introduction of private bills of incorporation by black legislators during the early years of Reconstruction for such black entities as building and loan associations is described in chapter 3, above. Black legislators continued this practice throughout the years they served in the state legislature. Most importantly, these private bills gave limited liability to black corporations just being established at the turn of the century. The significance of this power was revealed in 1899, during the last session in which blacks served in the state assembly and senate. That year, Thomas O. Fuller, who would hold the last black state senate seat for many decades, ran into difficulty when he introduced the bill to incorporate the North Carolina Mutual and Provident Association, the black-owned insurance company headquartered in Durham. White members of the state assembly, many of whom had no interest in giving black firms limited liability, nearly blocked Fuller's efforts.[28] This attitude would have a profound impact on blacks who were trying to incorporate educational, social, cultural, and business entities. During the 18 legislative sessions between 1868 and 1899 in which blacks held seats in the legislature, an average of 4.2 private bills of incorporation were passed for black organizations per session. By contrast, from 1901 to 1915, the first eight sessions in which no blacks served in the state assembly or senate, an average of only .75 bills aiding black organizations were passed per session.[29]

Although blacks landowners and businessmen who were elected to the state legislature held particularly visible positions, those who participated in local politics fulfilled an equally significant role. Enterprising blacks were represented in both groups of local black politicians: elected officials at the county and municipal level and those who held patronage jobs.

A profile of 41 blacks who served as either county commissioners or town aldermen during Reconstruction reveals that these elected officeholders were men of financial substance.[30] About one-third of these men owned real estate in 1870, and many of those who owned no land would start businesses or acquire land on which they would farm during the 1870s. Further, like members of their race who served in the state legislature during these years, a disproportionate share of these local officeholders were antebellum freedmen as well as mulattoes.[31]

Charles Blair served on the county commission of Chowan County at this time. In February 1867 Blair, a mulatto who kept a general store in Edenton, was one of the first blacks in North Carolina to be credit-rated. In 1869 he was considered to be "very attentive to business and a sober" individual. By the next year he had amassed $2,000 in real estate and $1,600 in personal estate.[32]

George Simmons, a county commissioner in Wayne County, had been a free mulatto before the war. In 1860 his $1,300 in property made him the second wealthiest free African American in Wayne County. By 1870, even though he was in his fifties and probably had transferred some of his estate to his children, Simmons still owned $370 in property, on which he farmed.

Frank Dancy, a mulatto county commissioner in Edgecombe County, was the son of one of the wealthiest postwar black landowners in the community, John Dancy Sr.[33] Although they were slaves before the war, the Dancys quickly emerged as one of the leading black families not only in Edgecombe but in the entire state. John Dancy Sr., a builder and contractor, also served as a county commissioner of Edgecombe.[34] In addition to being a county commissioner, Frank ran a very lucrative blacksmith firm for many years. In 1881 he reached the peak of his political career when, under very unusual circumstances, he became the first black mayor in North Carolina. At that time the county commissioners of Edgecombe County selected the mayor of Tarboro, the county seat. In 1881 the county commission comprised two white Democrats, two white Republicans, and two black Republicans. In addition to Frank Dancy, the other black Republican on the commission was the prominent businessman-politician Henry C. Cherry. Besides gaining his own vote, Dancy received the votes of Cherry and the two white Democrats, who preferred Dancy to either of the white Republicans.[35]

Although the Dancy family's political influence was based in Edgecombe County, it extended far beyond local politics. Frank's brother, John Jr., became one of the most influential social, economic, and political black leaders in North Carolina during the 1880s and 1890s.[36] John gained his first patronage office during the 1870s when John Hyman, the black merchant and congressman, recognizing the political influence of the Dancys in his congressional district, obtained John an appointment in the Sixth Auditor's Office of the Treasury Department in Washington D.C. After returning to North Carolina during the 1880s, John was elected registrar of deeds of Edgecombe twice. He held the distinction of attending the 1884 and 1888 Republican national conventions and seconding the nomination of General John A. Logan for vice-president at the former and John Sherman for president at the latter. In

1891 President Harrison appointed Dancy, who was at the time editor of the *Star of Zion,* the African Methodist Episcopal Zion newspaper, as the collector of customs in Wilmington. Although Dancy was removed from this very lucrative post for political reasons during President Cleveland's second term, in 1898, during President McKinley's administration, he regained this post by defeating John T. Howe, who had claimed his right to the position by virtue of his family's political influence and his residence in Wilmington. From 1901 to 1910 Dancy served as recorder of deeds of Washington D.C., a major patronage post open only to blacks of national political stature.

In addition to the county commissioners, those blacks who were elected to municipal office also were economic leaders in their communities. Some of the leading black aldermen of this era served in two of the state's largest cities, Wilmington and Raleigh. The financial status of Alfred Howe, John T. Howe's father, who served as both a city alderman of Wilmington and a county commissioner of New Hanover during Reconstruction, has already been described. One of Alfred Howe's fellow black alderman, William Kellogg, was just as wealthy. In 1860 Kellogg was a free mulatto wheelwright who owned $700 in property. By 1870, the year after he was elected to serve on the board of alderman, Kellogg had accumulated property valued at $3,500.[37]

James Lowrey, the credit-rated black carriage maker who advertised in 1877 that he had been in business for 30 years, was another prominent alderman in Wilmington. Although Lowrey may have been only a mediocre businessman, his involvement in politics brought him considerable economic success. By 1878 he was noted by a credit rater as earning "$1,200 per annum in the U.S. Customs House" in Wilmington, where he served as an inspector. Henceforth he was portrayed as a "very worthy colored man, said to be a good workman, who has occupied himself with politics and enjoyed an office in the Customs House which is a sinecure." Clearly, involvement in local politics and the rewards of elective and appointive office could enhance a black businessman's image.[38]

Three equally prominent blacks—Albert Farrar, Norfleet Dunston, and Stewart Ellison—served on the city commission of Raleigh during Reconstruction. In 1860 Farrar had been a free antebellum blacksmith with $450 in property. By 1870, the year after he began representing Raleigh's middle ward, he owned $1,000 in real estate. Dunston, a mulatto shoemaker who represented the city's western ward, also had been free before the war. He owned $700 in real estate and $300 in personal estate in 1870. Ellison, the alderman for the eastern ward, although born a slave, emerged as one of Raleigh's leading black businessmen during the 1870s and 1880s. Not only would he serve on the city commission for a number of terms but he would represent Wake County in the state assembly, and during the late 1880s and 1890s he would be chosen as the state Grand Master, the leader of black Masonry in North Carolina.

Black city officials in communities besides Wilmington and Raleigh also were local businessmen of distinction during Reconstruction. For example, Andrew J. Chesnutt, a member of the Fayetteville city commission, had been a free antebellum North Carolina mulatto. Sometime during the 1850s Andrew and his wife Ann had moved to Ohio, where their son, Charles, who would become one of North Carolina's most famous black authors, was born. After working as a teamster for the Union army during the war, Andrew decided to move to Fayetteville, where he helped establish a school for the Freedmen's Bureau. By 1869 he had opened a grocery store, which lasted throughout the 1870s. By 1870 he had acquired $500 in real estate and $200 in personal estate.[39]

Besides the salary and personal prestige they gained from office, black local officeholders could play a critical role in promoting the success of black economic enterprise in three ways. First, county commissioners and members of city councils had the power to sell unused public property. As illustrated in chapter 1 in the case of Edenton, black city commissioners often exercised this power in a way that resulted in a number of blacks' acquiring land. Second, black county and municipal officials could use their appointment power to see that blacks obtained such minor offices as timber and market inspectors and more important posts, such as members of the police and fire departments and coroner. A black undertaker or carpenter clearly would gain some additional money if he was also named coroner or wood inspector. Third, black county and city officers could determine tax policy and appoint the board of assessors and revenue collectors. Although a black assessor did not necessarily assess property belonging to another black at a more favorable rate and a black collector may not have been more forgiving to a delinquent black taxpayer, at least in such cases race was not, from the black perspective, the disadvantage it might have been had the assessor or collector been white. Moreover, for most blacks who felt that an error had been made in the assessment or collection process, it would be easier to ask for redress from a board at least partly composed of other blacks.

The importance of black local officeholders to black business became particularly evident during the 1870s for those blacks who sold liquor— more than one-fifth of all credit-rated black firms at the time. The politics surrounding the awarding of liquor licenses, which until 1877 were distributed largely by the popularly elected county and town commissioners, could be crucial to the success of the black businessmen. A teetotaling black grocer who enjoyed the favor of the local Republican organization could prevent a new black or white entrepreneur who planned to supplement his store's income by selling liquor from gaining a foothold. Likewise, those blacks who were engaged in the sale of liquor could always pull political strings in order to prevent a newcomer from obtaining a liquor license. This seems to have been one reason for the general success of J. A. Johnson, a 27-year-old mulatto who entered the Warrenton liquor trade in 1877, nearly a decade after blacks began selling alcohol in the community. His service on Warrenton's town council would only have aided his efforts.[40]

The important link between business, liquor, and politics became even more evident after 1877, when the Democrats pushed a new local government act through the legislature ending the direct election of most county and municipal officials and placing these positions under the control of justices of the peace. The justices of the peace were appointed by the legislature, which for the next 17 years was dominated by the Democrats.[41] That same year, the Democrats altered the election laws to make it very difficult for blacks to register and cast their votes for local offices.[42] Although it is impossible to document the direct link between their loss of local political control and the decline in their business fortunes, nearly half of the black firms dealing in liquor went out of business within two years of the passage of the new local government act.[43] For example, Charles Smith, a black businessman in Danbury, in Stokes County, had survived the depression of the mid 1870s but could not compete under the new law. Even though he started his confectionery and liquor business in June 1873 and amassed "a stock in trade" worth about $1,500, he was out of business by May 1879. In May 1878 he was recorded as being engaged only in "a little confectionery store," having "stopped the liquor traffic under a prohibitory law." Indeed, not only was the black liquor trade severely influenced by the new local government law but the overall development of black entrepreneurship seems to have slowed momentarily at the end of Reconstruction. Whereas the net number of black credit-rated firms in business grew by 4.0 firms per year between 1865 and 1875, over the next three years it advanced by only 1.7 firms per year.[44]

Between 1877 and 1894 the only local offices blacks were able to win were those that remained elective under the Democratic county government act—the county registrar of deeds and the county surveyor. It was not until 1895, when the Republicans and the Populists gained control of the state legislature and passed an act renewing the pre-1877 policy of having the voters directly elect most county and municipal officeholders and established a less partisan voter-registration and election process, that blacks again had the chance to hold other local offices. Hence, during the 1880s and early 1890s the rewards for local political influence shifted away from elective offices toward appointive posts. As long as the Republicans held the executive branch of the federal government and blacks were able to send Republicans to Congress to serve as their patrons, they would be rewarded for their local activity in support of the party by receiving posts. Patronage, of course, was neither an entirely new element for black politicians nor a link to black entrepreneurship. For example, in 1874, when Willis P. Moore, of Martin County, started a combination hotel, bar, and grocery enterprise, his effort was clearly aided by his being rewarded the postmastership of his community, Jamesville. In addition to bringing him an annual stipend of about $250, this primary patronage reward for political lieutenants at the local level, in Moore's case, as well as for other black merchants meant that both blacks and whites would have to come to black establishments to pick up their mail.[45]

Beginning in 1882 the patronage avenue of opportunity for blacks was widened considerably when the voters of the Second Congressional District, the "Black Second," as it was termed, used their district's black majority to elect three different blacks—James E. O'Hara, Henry P. Cheatham, and George H. White—to the U.S. House of Representatives for six of the next nine terms. Although John Hyman, the black representative from the district for one term, from 1875 to 1877, had used his influence to gain patronage positions for a few blacks, for example, John Dancy's position in the Treasury Department, his brief tenure in the House of Representatives did not allow him the opportunity to extend favor to many. Further, it was not apparent until the end of Hyman's term, when the Democrats rewrote the local government and election laws, that patronage posts would become far more viable than elective posts.

By far the most numerous patronage posts that could be dispersed to the party faithful were those linked to the postal system. Nearly every community in the state, from the smallest village to the largest city, had a postmastership that paid anywhere from a few hundred dollars to as much as $2,000.[46] In addition, the postmaster could appoint a clerk as an assistant, a post that paid a few hundred dollars. Further, the larger cities in North Carolina usually had letter carriers and railway postal clerks, whose salaries ranged from about $800 to about $1,000. Any of these positions could be a valuable supplement to one's income, and some paid well enough to be the sole source of income. One recipient of a postal-service position who used his patronage job to supplement his

business income was John M. Goode, of Charlotte, one of the few black
hotelkeepers in North Carolina. In 1891 Goode received the position of
letter carrier for Charlotte, which paid $850 a year.[47]

A sign of the importance of these postal jobs is that Congressmen
O'Hara, Cheatham, and White soon realized that their political prospects hinged on how successfully they dispersed this patronage to their
leading black supporters. Indeed, throughout the 1880s and 1890s the
black newspapers kept a tally of how many blacks gained such jobs and
made sure to give credit to these congressmen for their efforts. For example, in August 1897 the *Raleigh Gazette* termed Congressman White's
ability to obtain 20 postmasterships in his district and 36 total appointments for blacks during his first half-year in office as "an excellent show-
ing for our congressman."[48]

These patronage positions were often given in payment of distinct
debts congressmen owed to their supporters. For example, in 1889
Congressman Cheatham worked to obtain the postmastership of the
town of Wilson, which paid about $1,500, for Samuel Vick.[49] A graduate
of Lincoln University and the principal of a black public school, Vick
would soon marry Annie Washington, the daughter of one of Wilson's
most prominent antebellum free blacks, Jerry Washington. Further, Vick
would later serve two terms as Grand Master of the North Carolina black
Odd Fellows, the second most important black fraternal society in the
state. Despite his impressive civic credentials, Vick gained the postmastership because, as a Democrat from Wilson, John E. Woodard, observed,
"Cheatham owes Vick a political debt which he desires to pay off by having him appointed."[50] Woodard further described the reciprocal obligations that often accompanied acceptance of these patronage posts
when he added that Vick, in turn, had promised to make the wife of one
of Cheatham's "other political workers" his clerk. Whether Vick actually
fulfilled this promise is unclear. What is known is that he did appoint his
brother William to the position of clerk in the Wilson post office.[51]

Vick's selection of his brother as clerk indicates the role family ties
often played in patronage. Another example of how family links influenced patronage appointments is the case of George T. Wassom, who
in 1886 received a railroad postal clerk's position that paid $1,000
annually. Wassom had not only served as the chairman of the Wayne
County Republican executive committee but had worked to help his
brother-in-law, Congressman James O'Hara, gain election.[52]

Some blacks received patronage posts not because they had been involved in politics but simply because they knew the right people. For
example, in 1892 R. H. Henderson, of Fayetteville, a 26-year-old who
had only recently finished his medical studies at Howard University, re-

ceived the postmastership of Fayetteville, a position that paid $1,800 per year.[53] Henderson was recommended for the position by George C. Scurlock, one of Fayetteville's leading black politicians, as well as by Bishop James Hood, of the African Methodist Episcopal Zion Church. It did not hurt the young man that his father, Abraham Henderson, had been a leading mulatto businessman in Fayetteville since the 1870s.

Postal positions were especially desirable because they usually allowed the recipient to remain in his home community and therefore maintain his business; however, some of North Carolina's enterprising blacks were willing to move out of the state to receive patronage. For example, during the 1880s Matthew N. Leary, the affluent Fayetteville saddler, took a clerkship in the Pension Office in Washington D.C. that paid $1,000 per year. Soon after Leary left this post, he was replaced by a fellow townsmen and local Republican Party leader, George C. Scurlock. Scurlock, one of the state's few black attorneys, probably had determined that it was better to earn a steady income from the federal government than to try to make a living from a restricted local clientele.

Nevertheless, few black landowners and businessmen seem to have found it worthwhile to leave their hometowns to receive a patronage position. Even George Scurlock only remained in his Pension Office clerkship for a few years before resigning his post and returning to Fayetteville. After unsuccessfully running for North Carolina's Third District seat in the U.S. House of Representatives, Scurlock decided to pursue the district's major patronage position, Fayetteville's postmastership. Although his chances looked quite good in late 1891, they quickly soured. Rather than lose all input in the decision of who would be selected, Scurlock threw his support to R. H. Henderson. Within a few years, perhaps realizing the limits on his future political influence in Fayetteville, Scurlock moved to Greensboro and became a newspaper editor.

Even after the Republicans and Populists gained control of the state legislature and rewrote the local government and election laws in the mid 1890s, blacks were not elected to local office on the same scale as they had been during Reconstruction.[54] The Republican-Populist coalition was reluctant to nominate blacks for these offices because to do so opened their parties to Democratic false claims that their organizations were encouraging black dominance of local government. Indeed, even when they had the opportunity to do so, the Republicans and Populists often failed to reverse the trend Democrats had begun in 1877 and reintroduce a system of elections for local offices.

Even though they gained few elective local offices during the mid and late 1890s, blacks continued to gain patronage posts. As noted above, Congressman White was particularly effective in obtaining postal-service and other patronage offices for blacks. In addition, after their support in 1896 led to the election of a white Republican governor, Daniel Russell, black politicians cashed in their political chips by using the governor's aid to gain posts. For example, the son of the antebellum and postwar businessman Matthew Leary, John S. Leary, who had been instrumental in helping Russell first obtain the Republican nomination and later win the general election by carrying Mecklenburg County and especially the county seat, Charlotte, was not reluctant to request his reward. "While you had other friends here I am egotistic enough to say that but for my managing the convention proceedings you would have lost this county," Leary informed the governor-elect within weeks of the political victory. For Leary the only question was which post he should request, the postmastership of Charlotte or a position in the federal assay office.[55] In fact, he noted that the office he really wanted was that of assistant U.S. district attorney. Interested in Russell's thoughts about what post he should seek, Leary declared, "I am now in for a place for myself and I am going to rely upon you to help me in a large measure to get it." He added that Russell's "candor and straightforwardness" would play a major part in helping him "determine largely" his "future action."

Although the exact number of patronage positions held by North Carolina blacks during the mid to late 1890s will never be known since records on officeholding do not specify race, there is no question that the number of black officeholders, especially in postal-service positions, became a major thorn in the side of many whites. Two particular examples of how the appointment of black postmasters angered whites are the cases of Israel D. Hargett and Collin P. Anthony.

In July 1897 Israel D. Hargett, a schoolteacher, received the postmastership of Rocky Mount, in Edgecombe County, a post that paid $1,600. Hargett's appointment drew either strong support or opposition, largely based on race, from the residents of Rocky Mount. One of the most revealing complaints against Hargett, to which 75 residents, primarily merchants, attached their signatures, was that Hargett had "permitted the post office building to become the lounging place for the idlers and loafers of the community to the great inconvenience of the lady patrons of the office especially."[56] Apparently, Hargett required that patrons waiting for their mail stand in line in a sort of "bull pen arrangement," which white women found objectionable even though Hargett and his assistants were described by Thomas H. Battle, the white president of the Bank of Rocky Mount, as "people of good habits and character and not lacking in politeness."[57]

The character of Collin P. Anthony, another black postmaster, was held in lower regard than Hargett's. Despite having served as the registrar of deeds and a county commissioner of Halifax County as well as running a very successful bar, after being nominated for the postmastership of Scotland Neck, Anthony was charged with having fathered an illegitimate child. Although the former sheriff of Halifax came to Anthony's defense by asserting that he did not know of any man, "regardless of color, that enjoys a more enviable reputation than Mr. Anthony" and that he had never "heard one word or intimation, that would in the least reflect upon his good name for trust, honesty, efficiency, and morality," the U.S. Senate rejected Anthony's appointment. Anthony seems to have had the last word in the matter, because when another black received the appointment, Anthony's father-in-law posted the recipient's bond under the understanding that Anthony would serve as the chief clerk.[58]

Although North Carolina black landowners and businessmen, like all blacks, were victimized by the state constitutional amendment of 1900 requiring voters henceforth to be literate, the impact of this legislation on enterprising blacks needs to be placed in the perspective of post-1900 North Carolina politics. Black landowners and businessmen generally would not have been directly disfranchised by the amendment since most of them could read and write. Clearly, however, the political influence they had gained by virtue of the ballots cast by less affluent members of their race, most of whom were disfranchised, was lost. No black man, no matter how economically successful or well educated, could be elected to office without black voters. Of course, very few blacks were being elected to office during the mid to late 1890s, years when blacks voted under favorable electoral circumstances, since the Republican and Populist Parties were reluctant to place blacks on the ballot.

The more immediate political problem blacks faced as a result of disfranchisement was in the area in which they had been relatively successful, patronage. With the disfranchisement of blacks, the Republican Party lost any chance of electing one of its candidates to a statewide position that delivered patronage, such as the governorship. In addition, under these new political conditions no black could be elected to the U.S. House of Representatives and broker patronage as Congressmen O'Hara, Cheatham, and White had done so successfully during the 1880s and 1890s. Moreover, after the disfranchisement amendment was ratified, the white leadership of the Republican Party decided to make their organization "lily-white" in order to attract white voters; hence, the 6,145 blacks who still were registered two years later could not expect any patronage even if the Republicans won office. In 1905 the party made its position on patronage dispersal to blacks clear when its members in the state general assembly agreed not to recommend any blacks for appointment to public office and to remove any who already held a post.[59] The impact of the Republican Party's decision was immediate. A sample of 11 black postmasters in various communities in the Second Congressional District who were appointed in 1897 and 1898 reveals that none of these patronage recipients still held their offices ten years later.[60]

Some of the leading black political leaders who had built up strong contacts with the national Republican Party were able to weather the immediate storm. For example, as previously noted, James Young was able to use the influence he had gathered over more than two decades to gain a post as a federal tax collector, and John Dancy Jr., realizing that his days as collector of customs in Wilmington were numbered, decided to take the post as recorder of deeds of Washington D.C.

Some of the most prominent black businessmen also seem to have held onto their patronage. Berry O'Kelly, probably one of the state's wealthiest blacks, maintained his position in Method as postmaster, a position he had gained in 1891, through at least 1911. However, O'Kelly's success in holding on to this post was linked not so much to his affluence as to the fact that since Method was an overwhelmingly black community, the position did not carry the same symbolism that it would have carried in a more racially divided community.

Whether the political downturn adversely influenced the economic prospects of enterprising blacks is a complex question. Although the state tax commission records for the years just after disfranchisement indicate, as noted in chapter 1, that blacks increased their share of the real estate in the state and the city directories show steady growth in the number of black firms, these findings may be deceptive. Although it is valid to ask whether blacks were hurt economically by disfranchisement in any discernible way, the more valuable question might be whether blacks would have fared even better economically if they had not lost their political influence. In other words, would their gains have been even more substantial?[61] Again, there is firm evidence that once blacks no longer held seats in the state legislature, far fewer private bills aiding black enterprises were passed. Very likely blacks also faced more difficult circumstances at the county and municipal level. Finally, the question needs to be posed whether an attempt such as that led by Clarence Poe in 1915 to institute land segregation would have proceeded as far as it did if blacks had still been voting in large numbers and holding office.

5

Family, Marriage, and Education

ON 30 JANUARY 1972 John Clarence Scarborough Sr., one of Durham's leading black businessmen, died at the age of 93. Often during the years before his death Scarborough, a native of Kinston, North Carolina, related the circumstances that had prompted him to become a businessman. As a young man he had clerked for the prominent black Kinston grocer Wiley Lowrey, the brother of the Wilmington blacksmith and politician James Lowrey. When Scarborough's employer died in 1897 there was only a white-owned funeral home in Kinston. The white undertaker used a horse-drawn hearse for whites and a horse and wagon for blacks. Despite his stature in the community, Wiley Lowrey's friends could not convince the white undertaker to alter his policy and use the hearse for the funeral. Scarborough claimed that this incident had motivated him personally to do something about this "inequity."[1]

Scarborough was aided in his efforts by J. C. Hargett, who seems to have recognized something of himself in the young man. Hargett, born a slave in 1858, worked as a farm laborer until 1882, then moved to Kinston, where he started a mercantile business with only $60 in stock. Despite his modest beginnings, Hargett cleared a $5,000 profit in four years and emerged as one of the major black grocers in the town. By 1897 he was so influential in the community that he would have received the postmastership of the town had the Republicans not feared that his appointment might divide their party.[2]

Hargett sent Scarborough to Kittrell College in Kittrell, North Caro-

9. Scarborough Funeral Home. John Clarence Scarborough Sr. and his wife Daisy *(seated at left)* with employees and friends in front of the funeral home. (Courtesy of Durham Historic Photographic Archives, Durham County Library, Durham NC)

lina, obtained a rural mail route for him, and even supplied him with the horse and buggy the route required. Scarborough sealed his tie to the Hargetts when he married Hargett's daughter Daisy. Shortly after the turn of the century his father-in-law helped him realize his dream by financially backing Scarborough when he decided to start a funeral home in Kinston. In 1905, again with Hargett's assistance, Scarborough attended the Renouard Training School for Embalmers in New York City, where he was the only black member of his class of 27 students.

After leaving the Renouard School, Scarborough considered locating his business in Asheville, North Carolina, but he was persuaded by an agent of the North Carolina Mutual Life Insurance Company to base his new firm in Durham. Scarborough quickly established himself in Durham's black community by joining the Doric Masonic Lodge and the St. Joseph African Methodist Episcopal Church, institutions whose members included the city's prominent black business leaders. He served on St. Joseph's steward and trustee boards for more than fifty years. In addition, he became one of the first directors of the Mechanics and Farmers Bank and founded the Funeral Directors and Morticians Association of North Carolina. His major philanthropic achievement was his creation of the Scarborough Nursery Home in Durham to provide health-care and training for children whose parents worked.

Scarborough's entrepreneurial legacy did not end with his death, in 1972. Since from the very outset his funeral home business was run as a family enterprise, Scarborough's descendants maintained the firm after his retirement and death. Nearly one hundred years after the event that stimulated Scarborough to begin his business, the Scarborough Funeral Home, managed by Scarborough's grandson J. C. Scarborough III, remains one of Durham's major black enterprises.

Clearly, John Clarence Scarborough's business prospects were aided by the assistance he received from J. C. Hargett, and their relationship was strengthened when Scarborough married Hargett's daughter Daisy. The important role family ties played in shaping black economic success can be understood by investigating black marriage patterns.

Before the Civil War, slavery was the most influential factor affecting marriage for blacks. Although slave marriages were never upheld by law, scholars recognize the degree to which slaves felt their marriages were significant institutions.[3] If their masters were unwilling to let them find a spouse among the slaves owned by another master, then they had to choose their spouse from among the other slaves owned by their own masters.

Since they could move about with relatively few restrictions, free blacks had a much larger pool to choose from than did slaves; however, since more than 90 percent of the members of their race were enslaved in North Carolina, even free blacks' selection was limited. Few free blacks seem to have assumed the risks of marrying enslaved blacks.[4]

The tendency of whites to emancipate mulattoes rather than blacks further shaped antebellum spousal selection. The selection of spouses was limited in 1860, as nearly half of North Carolina's mulattoes were free compared with fewer than 3 percent of the state's blacks. Free mulatto men overwhelmingly married mulatto women largely because seven out of ten free African-American women were mulattoes. Black men were more than four times as likely to marry mulatto women as mulatto men were to marry black women (table 24). These marriage patterns did not result from differences in the economic opportunity of free blacks and mulattoes; roughly one-fifth to one-fourth of both black and mulatto freedmen owned real estate (table 25).[5]

Once the Civil War ended, economic factors replaced slavery as the most significant determinant of spousal selection. With the emancipa-

Table 24. Color of North Carolina Husbands and Wives, 1860 and 1870

Color of Husband/Wife	1860		1870	
	Number	Percent	Number	Percent
Black/black	719	74.1	45,784	95.3
Black/mulatto	251	25.9	2,245	4.7
Mulatto/mulatto	2,005	94.2	3,745	67.4
Mulatto/black	123	5.8	1,807	32.5

Source: Manuscript Census of the United States, 1860 and 1870, schedule 1, Alamance through Yancey Counties, North Carolina, Harold B. Lee Library, Brigham Young University, Provo UT.

Note: All of the information is based only on free male household heads. Since neither the 1860 nor the 1870 manuscript census enumerates familial relationships, I have assumed that a woman aged 15 or older who is listed immediately after the male household head and has the same surname was his wife. However, if a female's occupation is listed as "student" or "at home," the typical designation for a child of the household head, I did not consider her the male household head's wife.

Table 25. Real-Estate Ownership of Couples by Color, 1860 and 1870

Color of Husband/Wife	Percentage Who Owned Real Estate in	
	1860	1870
Black/black	21.0	5.0
Black/mulatto	23.5	13.0
Mulatto/mulatto	26.3	24.8
Mulatto/black	20.3	9.7

Source: Manuscript Census of the United States, 1860 and 1870, schedule 1, Alamance through Yancey Counties, North Carolina, Harold B. Lee Library, Brigham Young University, Provo UT.

tion of over 330,000 slaves, 93.0 percent of whom were black, the process of selecting a spouse was bound to change. However, in the short
term the vast majority of blacks had black spouses, and the overwhelming
majority of mulattoes had mulatto spouses, because most blacks and mulattoes who were married as of 1870 had been married before slavery
ended.

Antebellum economic status clearly shaped spousal selection in the
immediate postwar years. Whereas blacks in 1870 were only one-fourth
as likely to own land as free blacks in 1860, mulattoes experienced
a much smaller decline in economic status. Whereas 25.7 percent of
free mulattoes had owned land in 1860, 19.5 percent did so in 1870
(table 1). Significantly, the color of both spouses influenced whether
the couple owned real estate in 1870. Black husbands with black wives
were the least likely to own land. In fact, they were only one-fifth as likely
to own land as mulatto husbands with mulatto wives. Clearly their economic status was the result of most of them having only become free
since the end of the war. By contrast, black husbands with mulatto wives
were two and one-half times as likely as black husbands with black wives
to own land (table 25). The difference between the economic condition of black husbands with mulatto wives and that of black husbands
with black wives probably resulted from the combination of two factors:
one, since half of the mulatto women were free before the war, many of
these women had had the opportunity to gain some property that they
could bring into marriage; two, mulatto women, coming from a relatively
higher economic status, may have been attracted to black men who
owned property. Supporting the latter possibility is the fact that mulatto
husbands with black wives were slightly less likely to own land than black
husbands with mulatto wives and far less likely than mulatto husbands
with mulatto wives (table 25). Therefore, although during the immediate postwar years spousal selection seems to have been shaped by skin
color, the primary factor actually was economic status resulting from the
disproportionate prewar emancipation of mulattoes and the head start
this emancipation provided mulattoes in accumulating property.

The opportunity of most African Americans to gain property would
be linked to the intermarriage of the mulatto and black populations,
although this process was impeded by the distinct economic differences
that existed between these two groups. The 1880 census was the last
statewide record in which the color of husbands and wives was enumerated. Despite its limitations, a sample of half of the African-American
husbands and wives in North Carolina in 1880 indicates the pace of integration of these two groups (table 26). Keeping in mind that most of

Table 26. Couples by Color, 1860–80

Color of Husband/Wife	1860	1870	1880	1880 Husbands under Age 25
Black/black	73.9%	95.3%	92.3%	91.4%
Black/mulatto	26.1	4.7	7.7	8.6
Mulatto/mulatto	94.2	67.5	65.6	61.8
Mulatto/black	5.8	32.5	34.4	38.2

Source: Manuscript Census of the United States, 1860, 1870, and 1880, schedule 1, North Carolina, Harold B. Lee Library, Brigham Young University, Provo UT.
Note: The 1880 sample includes every African-American household headed by a man in Alamance through Jackson Counties who was married to a black or a mulatto woman.

the 1880 couples had been married for many years and therefore did not have the postwar opportunity to marry someone whose skin color differed, it is not surprising that most of the couples at that point in time were married to someone enumerated as having the same skin color. However, an examination of those husbands under age 25, men who married during the mid to late 1870s, indicates that these men were more likely than previously married men to select a bride with either lighter or darker skin than their own.

The process of integration of black and mulatto landowning and non-landowning families appears to be even more dynamic on the local level. Between 1867 and 1880 in Johnston County 32 men whose parents owned real estate married.[6] In 26 of these marriages the bride's parents did not own real estate. Hence, in eight out of ten cases the lower economic status of the potential bride's parents did not deter the groom or his parents.

Grooms from landowning families in Johnston County may have been willing to marry brides whose families did not own real estate largely because most of these men's families were small landowners. Indeed, the parents of only 2 of the 32 grooms owned more than $500 in real estate. In fact, these two exceptions, John and Willis Evans, were brothers whose father, Clemons, a free antebellum landowning farmer, owned real estate valued at $600 in 1870. Furthermore, more than one-third of the grooms came from families who owned less than $100 in land.[7] When York and Venus Watson, who farmed land valued at only $75, saw their two sons, Thomas and York Jr., marry women whose parents owned no land, they had no reason to view their sons as marrying women whose economic status was much below their own.

In selecting spouses, Johnston County women from landowning families appear to have been nearly as likely to marry grooms from non-landowning families as they were to marry grooms from landowning families. Eight of the 14 women whose families owned land in 1870 (57.1%) chose husbands whose families did not own land. Significantly, there was no relationship between the value of land their parents owned and the likelihood of brides marrying grooms from non-landowning families; in fact, all three of the women whose parents owned more than $300 in land selected husbands whose parents owned no land.

Many of those grooms who came from families that owned no land seem to have fared well after their marriages to women whose parents owned real estate. For example, on 17 December 1874 Henry H. Smith, whose parents owned no land, married Martha Thomas, the daughter of John and Amanda Thomas, the owners of $400 in real estate. By 1882 Henry Smith had acquired 36 acres worth $300, and by 1890 his land was valued at $900.[8] His in-laws also prospered during these same years. Although Martha's father had died by 1890, her mother owned land worth $550 that year. Further, Martha's two brothers, Daniel and Brasswell, owned real estate with a combined total value of $3,020, and Daniel was acting as an agent for three unmarried female relatives whose total land was valued at $1,830. Therefore, perhaps property-owning families accepted their daughters' marrying men from propertyless families because they recognized that such unions would not necessarily diminish their economic position.

Although property ownership may not have been a prohibitive barrier against the integration of families in overwhelmingly rural communities like Johnston County, were the prospects similar in urban centers? For most of the early postwar years this issue was relatively unimportant as most blacks in North Carolina resided in the countryside. However, during the 1890s and the first 15 years of the twentieth century, when cities in the state experienced substantial growth, among enterprising blacks, many of whom increasingly were well-educated professionals, there appears to have developed a more exclusive character. The nature of this group's self-awareness can be viewed most clearly in the city of Charlotte, whose black business sector grew tremendously from the 1890s through 1915 as the community emerged as the largest city in the state.

The most obvious symbol of the new self-perception among Charlotte's elite blacks was the emergence of social clubs. The first of these social clubs to be mentioned in newspapers was the Montauk Social

League of Charlotte, which held a banquet in the city at the end of
1898.[9] The banquet was held over the Queen City Pharmacy, one of the
leading black firms in the community. Those in attendance at the Social
League banquet included many of the city's prominent black professionals and businessmen such as John S. Leary, one of the state's major black
attorney-politicians, and a number of the city's black doctors: G. L. Black-
well, W. H. Graves, John Harris, N. B. Houser, J. W. Smith, William H.
Vick, George W. Williams, and A. A. Wyche. Many of these men were
active in the two black Masonic lodges in Charlotte. Some of these doctors had had close ties with one another even before they took up their
practices in Charlotte. For example, both Williams and Wyche had
graduated from the Leonard Medical School of Shaw University two
years earlier, and Graves had finished his studies at that institution just
one year earlier.[10] Solidifying their professional bond, within a few
months the doctors and pharmacists would create the Queen City Medical and Pharmaceutical Society in order to coordinate the efforts of
Charlotte's black medical community.[11]

Another elite black social organization in Charlotte was the Friday Af-
ternoon Club, known for its annual gala events. For example, on a Friday
evening in February 1915 the club met at the "handsome residence" of
Dr. and Mrs. John Eagles on Caldwell Street and held "the largest and
most brilliant social affair of the mid-winter season."[12] Dr. Eagles, the son
of a John S. W. Eagles, a landowning Wilmington carpenter who had
represented New Hanover County in the North Carolina state house
during Reconstruction, after graduating from the Leonard School of
Pharmacy of Shaw University in 1894 opened one of the major black
drugstores in the city. Among the members of the club were many of the
city's black doctors, ministers, and educators.

In addition to these social clubs, a number of black literary societies
composed of members of the black elite arose in the city. The most
notable of these was the Pierian Literary Circle, which was created in
1899. In 1902 the Pierian held a banquet attended by 35 couples.[13] The
affluence of the members was hinted at in the description of their at-
tire: "The ladies in silk, satin . . . with here and there pearls and dia-
monds, rubies, sapphires, opals, emeralds, gold and bouquets, and the
gentlemen in evening dress—they presented a picturesque scene." The
correspondent who wrote about the event proudly emphasized that such
black institutions of higher education as Biddle, Livingstone, Tuskegee,
Shaw, Howard, Lincoln, Benedict, Scotia, and the Virginia Theological
Seminary and College were represented by the members, who included
college and university professors, ministers, medical and dental doctors,

lawyers, pharmacists, editors, insurance agents, printers, stenographers, bookkeepers, dressmakers, and teachers, as well as a number of college and university undergraduates. Besides holding banquets, the Pierian subscribed to the major magazines and journals of the era for its members' reading pleasure. The popularity of the Pierian led to the formation of at least three other black literary circles—the Puskin, the Paradise, and the John S. Whittier—which read and discussed works by Shakespeare and other writers.[14]

The black elite of Charlotte also frequently convened for private socials and parties unrelated to formal organizations. For example, on the evening of 16 August 1909, "the pleasant custom among Charlotte's elite society of inviting friends to meet friends" led a number of guests to gather at the home of Miss Bertha Blake in order to listen to solos by Miss Pearl Wimberly, of Augusta, Georgia, and to meet visitors from communities as far away as Mobile, Alabama, and Savannah, Georgia.[15]

One of the most important social events of the elite black community of Charlotte was the twenty-fifth-anniversary party of Mr. and Mrs. John Crockett in January 1915.[16] John Crockett, the general secretary and manager of the Afro-American Mutual Insurance Company and editor of the *Progressive Messenger,* a black-operated newspaper, was described as a member "in the first rank of North Carolina black businessmen." During Crockett's 19 years in the city, "through thrift and economy" he had "accumulated a splendid amount of residential property." Among those invited to this event, which was "pronounced by many capable judges to be one of the finest and most elaborate social events in the history of colored Charlotte," were the black community's "leading men and women in every profession and calling." The couple received numerous gifts, most in the form of silver, from prominent residents of Charlotte and other North Carolina cities as well as from friends in Virginia and South Carolina.

Although rarely as ostentatious as the Crockett anniversary gala, the weddings of Charlotte's elite society also highlighted the developing self-perception of enterprising blacks. In June 1915 the city witnessed the marriage of one of its most prominent young women, Miss Emma R. Wyche, to Dr. R. William G. Capel.[17] Emma, a schoolteacher, had attended Scotia Seminary, the Presbyterian black women's educational institution that proudly claimed to be the "Mount Holyoke of the South." Dr. Capel, a native of Rockingham County and a graduate of Biddle University, in Charlotte, had located his dentistry practice in Huntington, West Virginia. Emma was escorted down the aisle of the Emmanuel Congregational Church by her uncle, Dr. A. A. Wyche, one of Charlotte's most eminent black doctors. "Many costly and serviceable gifts" were received by the couple, including the deed of a city lot from Emma's brother Albert.

The social climate of enterprising blacks in Charlotte clearly suggests the increasingly important role higher education played for members of this group during the late nineteenth and the early twentieth century. To what degree, then, was higher education accessible to North Carolina blacks, and what economic opportunities accompanied it?

The 50 years following the Civil War witnessed the establishment of a number of higher-education institutions for black North Carolinians. For most of this period the various church denominations played a dominant role in the creation of these schools. Following the founding of Shaw University in Raleigh in 1865 by the American Baptist Home Mission Society, six other church-sponsored colleges were founded before the end of the century: St. Augustine's College in Raleigh (1867), by the Episcopalians; Biddle College in Charlotte, for men (1867), and Scotia Seminary in Concord, for women (1867), by the Presbyterian Board of Missions for Freedmen; Bennett College in Greensboro (1873), by the Freedmen's Aid Society of the Methodist Episcopal Church; Livingstone College in Salisbury (1883), by the African Methodist Episcopal Zion Church; and Kittrell College in Kittrell (1886), by the African Methodist Episcopal Church.[18]

Given the racial situation in North Carolina and the speed with which the Democrats gained control of the state legislature during Reconstruction, it is not surprising that public-supported black institutions lagged far behind church-supported colleges. The first public college for blacks, Fayetteville State, was not created until 1877, and it would be another decade and a half before three other black colleges gained state funds: Elizabeth City State and North Carolina Agricultural and Mechanical (later North Carolina A&T), both in 1891, and Winston-Salem State in 1892. Further, it would be 1910 before another black institution, North Carolina Central, would gain state support. Significantly, except for North Carolina Agricultural and Mechanical, none of the public-supported institutions were true colleges; rather, their primary function was to teach secondary-level students and to train teachers. Nearly 90 percent of the college students who graduated from North Carolina institutions attended one of the seven denominational colleges.[19]

Although church membership clearly influenced which denominational college a student attended, in general undergraduates selected the college located closest to their homes. For example, listings of the student bodies of Shaw during the mid 1870s and St. Augustine's during the early 1880s indicate that most of the students were residents of communities of the eastern piedmont or the coastal plain, which were within a single day's travel of the two Raleigh institutions. Likewise, the North Carolina students at Biddle during the early 1880s tended to come from communities in the western piedmont in the general vicinity of Charlotte.[20] Students may have chosen to attend the denominational colleges near their homes because there was relatively little difference between the costs of the colleges, as the institutions did not calculate tuition based on whether a student was a member of the sponsoring church. In fact, between 1865 and 1915 the fees for undergraduates at all seven of these private colleges remained fairly constant at between $6 and $8 a month for tuition, room, and board. Usually three-fourths of the fee went toward room and board. Further, the colleges seem to have followed a similar academic calendar, beginning in October and ending in May.[21]

Since the primary purpose of black denominational colleges was to train ministers and teachers, all seven of the private institutions offered either an undergraduate or a postgraduate program in theology, and five of the seven maintained a normal program for students seeking teaching certificates. Most normal students matriculated through either a 2- or a 3-year terminal program, but some chose to continue their education by entering the college program in order to receive a bachelor's degree.[22]

The bachelor's degree programs at all of the institutions emphasized a strong liberal arts curriculum. For example, during the 1870s and 1880s undergraduates at Shaw were required to take three years of Latin and two years of Greek, mental, moral, and natural philosophy, mathematics courses consisting of algebra, geometry, and trigonometry, and science classes in physiology, botany, chemistry, and zoology.[23]

Despite their similar costs, academic calendars, and curriculums, the seven denominational institutions varied in the mixture of programs they offered. For example, during its early years Scotia Seminary appears to have been largely a grammar and preparatory school for women. Although it did offer a normal program for training teachers, it would not become a true college until 1916.[24] Bennett also was primarily a preparatory school for most of its infancy; indeed, the school would not grant its initial bachelor's degree until 1885, 12 years after its creation. Over the following 25 years it averaged fewer than six graduates a year.[25]

The last of these denominational institutions to be created, Kittrell seems to have realized quickly that it could best succeed by specializing as a normal school. Therefore, during its first two decades it awarded 151 normal degrees and only 2 bachelor's degrees.[26] Although Livingstone also maintained a very large normal program, granting 280 normal degrees between 1885 and 1905, it also offered a strong college department. By 1905 it had granted 54 bachelor's degrees as well as 24 master's degrees and 1 doctorate.[27]

Biddle was overwhelmingly a liberal arts college. In fact, in 1877 it became the first black college in North Carolina to grant a bachelor's degree. By 1915 it had granted a total of 199 bachelor's degrees. Because it was exclusively a men's institution, Biddle chose not to have a normal program (at most other institutions the normal program largely served women). However, Biddle maintained the largest theology program of any black college in the state; by 1915 it had granted 164 postgraduate theology degrees.[28]

St. Augustine's maintained the most balanced ratio between normal and college students: by 1915 it had granted 116 normal and 108 bachelor's degrees. The institution also trained a number of clergymen in its theology department, many of whom were jointly enrolled in the college department. In addition, the institution offered a very large grammar and preparatory program, as well as degrees in various trades and nursing. Indeed, indicative of the institution's diverse programs, in 1917 only 16 of its 473 students matriculated in the college, and only 30 attended the normal school.[29]

Throughout the period from 1865 to 1915 Shaw was the dominant black educational institution in North Carolina. Because the college was coeducational from its inception and therefore had a much larger undergraduate student body than that of all-male Biddle, it granted far more bachelor's degrees. By 1905 a total of 142 students had received a bachelor's degree from Shaw, compared with 76 from Biddle.[30] In addition to its coeducational undergraduate program, Shaw also offered women degrees in its Estey Seminary and its normal school. Further, it maintained a fairly large undergraduate program in theology for men. Finally, Shaw's stature as the preeminent black denominational university in the state was solidified by the creation of a medical school in 1885 and a law school in 1886. Since no other denominational college had such professional programs, by 1914, when Shaw closed its medical and law schools, 432 medical, 134 pharmaceutical, and 54 law degrees had been awarded by the university.[31]

What was the background of black North Carolinians who attended college during these years? The lists of college students from this period indicate that the exceptionally affluent black parents easily could afford to give their children the advantages of higher education. An outstanding example of a family having this capability is the Taylors of Wilmington.[32] Henry Taylor, a freeborn mulatto house carpenter, was the wealthiest African-American landowner in New Hanover County in 1870. In Wilmington he was a founder of both the Chestnut Presbyterian Church and the Giblem Masonic Lodge, the second black Masonic lodge in the state.

Taylor could afford to send his elder son, John, to the most prestigious black institution in the nation, Howard University. With the advantages of this education and his family's wealth, in Wilmington John was also able to run a real-estate firm and a shoe store, to serve as president of a building and loan association, and to be appointed deputy collector of customs. John, in turn, could afford to send at least two of his children to Fisk University.

Henry Taylor's younger son, Robert, was the first black to graduate from the Massachusetts Institute of Technology, where he was the class valedictorian, in 1892. While studying architecture at MIT, Robert was visited twice by Booker T. Washington, who wanted the young man to teach at and design the campus of Tuskegee Institute. Robert accepted this offer and supervised the construction of at least 22 buildings at Tuskegee, including Booker T. Washington's home, The Oaks.

Although there is no record that Henry Taylor's two daughters, Anna Maria and Sarah Louise, attended college, they married two very prominent men and provided their children with excellent educations. Anna Maria's husband, Dr. James Francis Shober, a graduate of Lincoln University of Pennsylvania and the Howard Medical School, is credited as the first black doctor to pass the North Carolina Board of Medical Examiners examination. Sarah Louise's husband, John Whiteman, was one of the leading black entrepreneurs in Wilmington. Anna Maria and Sarah Louise's eight children attended Fisk University, Howard University, Hampton Institute, Tuskegee Institute, Johnson C. Smith University (formerly Biddle College), Shaw University, and the Wharton School of Finance of the University of Pennsylvania.

Although probably better off financially than most blacks, the typical black college student from North Carolina definitely was not as wealthy as the Taylors. For example, fewer than one-fifth of Shaw undergraduate men during the mid to late 1870s came from families who owned real estate in 1870.[33] The median value of land owned by even these landowning families was only $250. Although this was about three times as much as the average black real-estate holding statewide, given the costs of attending college it is remarkable that it was not even higher. Although the $8 monthly it cost to attend college may seem nominal, we must remember that even black families who owned land generally possessed only a few hundred dollars' worth. Therefore, the $250 to $300 required to educate a single son or daughter for four years must have been a substantial sacrifice for even black landowning families.

Because of this financial sacrifice faced by the families of college students, North Carolina's black denominational institutions encountered the common problem of retaining students. This problem seems to have been particularly acute during difficult financial periods, especially during the depressions of the mid 1870s and the early 1890s. Fewer than one-fourth of Shaw's undergraduates enrolled during the 1876–77 academic year and only about one-third of those enrolled during the 1891–92 academic year eventually graduated from the college. By contrast, during better times it was common for two-thirds, and not unusual for four-fifths, of all undergraduates who began attending a college to receive their bachelor's degree. For example, 72.7 percent of Livingstone's and 79.1 percent of Shaw's undergraduates during the mid 1890s graduated at the turn of the century.[34]

The records of the various colleges indicate that although numerous students were entering college, there was a distinct attrition with each year of attendance. For example, during the 1882–83 academic year there were 31 undergraduates at Biddle: 13 freshmen, 9 sophomores, 5 juniors, and 4 seniors. This pattern of attrition was even more pronounced for the undergraduates at Livingstone during the 1895–96 academic year: 9 freshmen, 3 sophomores, 2 juniors, and no seniors. Although those who made it to their junior and senior years overwhelmingly graduated, few could afford to matriculate that long.[35]

Hence, while some college education was available for many blacks, few could afford to take advantage of the opportunity long enough to receive a degree. Nevertheless, this was an era in which a college degree was not absolutely necessary in order to live a comfortable life. In fact, because of the large number of normal programs for training teachers, many of the college students during this era already were teachers. For example, half of the students at Biddle taught primary school during some portion of the 1882–83 academic year. Collectively these students taught a total of 220 months and earned more than $5,000 in salary. This level of work and amount of compensation is remarkable because Biddle, as one of the few schools without a normal program, probably had a much smaller pool of students who were teaching while attending the institution. Further, given the short public-school academic year in North Carolina and the inferior pay black teachers received, that the Biddle students could have averaged nearly $70 in salary from their teaching, enough to pay their annual educational expenses, is remarkable. What is equally impressive given the fact that most of Biddle's graduates would eventually choose careers in the ministry or education is that so many chose to complete their college degrees instead of teaching full-time.[36]

The financial difficulties faced by black college students and the role of their teaching in helping them to reach their educational goals is best illustrated by the experience of Thomas Fuller, the only black North Carolina state senator at the time of disfranchisement.[37] Fuller's father, Henderson, was a black carpenter and wheelwright who while he was a slave built houses by contract, hiring his time from his master. He also learned to read while in bondage. After the Civil War Henderson bought a piece of property in Franklin County that by 1870 was valued at $800. During Reconstruction he was an active Republican and served as a magistrate.

As a child Thomas, the youngest of 13 children, attended private schools. In 1882 he began to attend the state-sponsored normal school in Franklinton, and he entered Shaw University in 1885. Despite his father's ownership of property, Thomas, like many Shaw students, needed to work while taking classes. He began as a sweeper and later was placed in charge of the school's reading room. He invested in cakes, which he sold to fellow students who were hungry between meals. He also made money privately teaching students and barbering them.

Despite his creative efforts to stay secure financially, Thomas found himself short of funds and in debt for board and tuition. He would have left school to work if Shaw's president, Henry Martin Tupper, had not encouraged him to stay. Because of his previous teaching experience he received the post of assistant teacher from the American Baptist Home Mission Society. His earnings from this position allowed him to continue at Shaw and earn his bachelor's degree in 1890 and a master's degree in 1893. After receiving his undergraduate degree, Thomas began his career as a full-time teacher and minister. When a Republican nominee was needed to fill the state senate seat for the Warren and Vance County district in 1898, Thomas was given the nomination and easily won the election.

In deciding to pursue careers in both education and the ministry before serving his single term in the state senate Thomas Fuller was following the typical occupational route for men who received college degrees. Nearly two-fifths of the 443 men who received college degrees from Biddle, Livingstone, St. Augustine's, and North Carolina Agricultural and Mechanical College through 1915 became members of the clergy. About half as many in this 4-school sample became educators. If to these we add men whose careers combined both education and the ministry, then two-thirds of all male graduates worked in education and/or the clergy.[38]

After education and the ministry, the next most common occupation, medicine, was pursued by 13.1 percent of male college graduates.[39] Interestingly, those who went into medicine were not predisposed to enter that profession because of their family background. Indeed, many of the men who became doctors and pharmacists seem to have been sons of men who began as craftsmen. For example, one family that sent a number of children to college and produced three doctors was the Dardens of Wilson.[40] According to family legend, in 1868 14-year-old Charles Henry Darden walked into the town of Wilson. He arrived with no money or friends, but he evidently had gained some mechanical skills. After first earning a living by traveling door to door repairing locks and sharpening knives, he opened a small repair shop on the main street of Wilson. Once his business began to prosper, he was able to marry Dianah Scarborough, the daughter of a couple who had been freeborn and who owned a small confectionery store in Wilson. Charles diversified his trade by making coffins, starting a funeral establishment, and running a produce store.

Although Charles never received a formal education, he was determined that his 13 children would. Because Wilson did not have a high school for blacks, Charles sent 10 of his children away to communities that did. Fittingly, when Wilson finally did build a black high school years later, it was named Charles H. Darden High.

John, Charles Darden's eldest son, attended high school in Salisbury, worked his way through Livingstone College, from which he earned a normal degree in 1895, and received his medical degree from the Leonard Medical School at Shaw University in 1901. Since Wilson already had a black physician, John chose to move to Opelika, Alabama, where he was the only black doctor in a 30-mile radius. Having learned from his father that diversification could ensure success, in addition to his medical practice John opened a drugstore in Opelika. His decision to begin this firm may have been prompted by the fact that Charles Darden's third son, James Benjamin, had just earned his degree in pharmacy from Howard University. The two brothers were partners in the drugstore in Opelika until James, with John's encouragement, left to attend Meharry Medical School in Nashville, Tennessee. After his graduation James practiced medicine in Petersburg, Virginia.

Because John and James had moved out of state and the second son, Charles, had left home long before, when Charles Darden retired his business interests in Wilson were taken over largely by his fourth and fifth sons, Camillus and Arthur. Although Camillus decided that it was not worth leaving Wilson to attend either high school or college, he did gain a degree from mortuary science school. In 1908 Arthur received a bachelor's degree in agriculture from North Carolina Agricultural and Mechanical College, and later he too attended mortuary school. The two brothers ran a funeral business in Wilson for many years.

Charles Darden's sixth son, Russell, graduated from Biddle University and went on to attend Howard University Law School. During a Christmas vacation trip, however, he died of pneumonia in Harlem, New York. Walter, the seventh son and youngest child, after his mother's death spent much of his youth living with his brother John in Opelika. He went on to graduate from Howard University and, like two of his brothers, became a doctor. He established his practice in Newark, New Jersey.

The pattern John, James, and Walter Darden established of practicing medicine in communities other than their hometown was quite common. For example, Ned Alston, a landowning harnessmaker and stablekeeper in Louisburg, had two sons, Marcus and Jesse, graduate from the Leonard Medical School. After completing his studies in 1890, Marcus chose to practice medicine in Charlotte. Jesse graduated as a pharmacist in 1894 and established a drugstore in Alabama.[41] Fewer than one-fifth of the North Carolina graduates of Leonard Medical School during the institution's first twenty years became doctors or pharmacists in their home communities.[42] Those who did return to their hometowns generally were from large cities like Charlotte or Raleigh, both of which could sustain more than one black doctor.

After medicine the next most popular occupation pursued by college graduates was business. However, only 11.3 percent of college graduates went into business.[43] It may be that few college graduates followed business careers because during the late nineteenth century most of the North Carolina blacks who became businessmen recognized no need to have a college degree in order to succeed. A liberal arts education and a college degree were not nearly as important assets for black merchants as a thorough knowledge of their customers' ability to pay their bills. This was particularly the case when most merchants conducted their firms in villages and small towns, where it was possible to have an intimate knowledge of their clients.

J. W. Stitt, who graduated from Biddle College in 1895 and became a merchant in Winston-Salem, was the first black North Carolina college graduate in the 4-school sample who became a businessman. Although only 4.2 percent of the students who graduated before the end of the century followed Stitt's course, 14.7 percent of the post-1900 graduates entered the business sector.[44]

Perhaps the improved business climate for blacks after the turn of the century, as demonstrated by the higher rates of persistence for black firms after 1900, enticed more black college students into business careers (table 18). Further, since so many black doctors found it necessary to practice their skills away from their hometowns or even out of state, clearly there was a limit to the demand for college-educated black professionals. Business was becoming a relatively attractive alternative career option for men with college degrees.

An additional reason why college-educated men increasingly entered business at the turn of the century may have had to do with the changes the North Carolina economy was experiencing. Since a larger share of the black merchants, like J. W. Stitt, were establishing their firms in cities like Winston-Salem, in the newly developed piedmont, a section that lacked the historic intimacy of the villages and small towns of eastern North Carolina, a college degree may have provided some benefit. As previously noted in the case of Charlotte, the preeminent developing piedmont city, an individual's educational attainment in a large city often influenced his or her social status, which in turn could create favorable economic opportunity. Therefore, a college degree may have served as a valuable passport in this new business and community environment.

The North Carolina Agricultural and Mechanical College was exceptional in that it was the one North Carolina institution whose graduates generally followed occupational paths linked to business. More than two-fifths of the institution's alumni received training to become mechanics, architects, or engineers or to perform other skilled trades. An additional number of its graduates were engaged directly in the financial sector of the economy. For example, Charles Amey, a member of the class of 1903, was employed by the Mechanics and Farmers Bank of Durham. Charles Donnell, of the class of 1907, and Edward Merrick, of the class of 1908, who later became brothers-in-law, after leaving North Carolina Agricultural and Mechanical worked for the North Carolina Mutual Life Insurance Company and eventually became members of its board of directors. Even more of the college's graduates would have become skilled artisans and businessmen if they had not been enticed to teach their skills at technical colleges and institutions.[45]

The reason why college-educated blacks pursued a career in business rather than a profession is best exemplified by Arthur J. Clement, a 1905 graduate of Biddle College.[46] After receiving his bachelor's degree, Clement, the son of former slaves who became landowners in Rowan County after the Civil War, started working in Charlotte for the People's Benevolent Relief Association, a small black insurance company. Apparently, Clement took this job in order to save enough money to attend the Leonard Medical School of Shaw University. After the People's Benevolent Relief Association was taken over by the North Carolina Mutual Life Insurance Company in 1906, Clement was assigned by his new employer as superintendent of the firm's Charleston District in South Carolina. Clement found so much success with North Carolina Mutual, a company that from its inception demonstrated a preference for employees who had received a higher education, that he continued to work there until his retirement in 1949.[47]

The most unifying characteristic of family, marriage, and educational patterns of enterprising blacks was the degree to which this group's ranks were open to newcomers. J. C. Hargett's sponsorship of J. C. Scarborough's educational and occupational endeavors and his allowing the young man to become his son-in-law is indicative of this fluid economic and social environment. The gradual intermarriage of mulattoes and blacks and the fact that so many landowning families welcomed in-laws from non-landowning backgrounds further illustrate this fluidity.

Although higher education held the potential to create firmer social boundaries as it increasingly emerged as a defining attribute of enterprising blacks and their children, what is striking is the degree to which a higher education was available to a wide spectrum of North Carolina blacks. If the wealthiest black families in the postwar years ensured viable career options for their children by providing them with a college education, so too did many black families who had been slaves a generation before and who had not been fortunate enough to emerge from the immediate postwar years as property owners. Since no black family as late as 1915 could point to an ancestor who had been a college graduate before 1865, postbellum higher-education attainment appears to have been an achievement uniting rather than dividing blacks from diverse economic roots.

Epilogue

THIS STUDY of enterprising blacks in North Carolina between 1865 and 1915 questions scholars' tendency to portray the experience of southern blacks after the Civil War in monolithic terms. Although racism clearly was a fact of life that blacks shared during this era and one that surely influenced their level of economic success, all blacks did not experience racism in the same way. In the area of landholding, African Americans who were free before the war, and especially those who had light skin and skills, were in a far more favorable position to take advantage of emancipation than the vast majority who were not liberated until the arrival of the Union army or the end of the conflict.

The economic opportunities open to blacks also varied largely according to the environment in which they chose to live. Although residents in both the countryside and the cities experienced a slow but steady increase in the share of land they owned, the towns and cities had a much more flexible land market. Blacks who attempted to purchase farmland simply were competing with one another for a commodity that did not grow as quickly as did the demand for it.

The diversity of the black experience was particularly evident in the business sector. Most black entrepreneurs had no choice but to compete against one another for a clientele that was predominantly black and had a quite limited purchasing power. As a result of these conditions, which were largely anchored in racism, most black businessmen were bound to fail. But such was also the fate of most white businessmen. What is re-markable is the degree to which a significant segment of the black busi-ness community, through a combination of personal character and an ability to adjust to market forces, survived and in many cases thrived.

This study of enterprising blacks in North Carolina also highlights the relationship between economic success and political participation. Al-though the right to hold office and vote clearly aided blacks' economic endeavor, the absence of both never entirely could destroy it.

Finally, the history of enterprising blacks is the story of the creation of an identity. Blacks who acquired land and conducted businesses were constantly cited by blacks and whites alike as extraordinary individuals. Their exceptional situation gave them a distinct status, but one that con-tained two interesting paradoxes. Not only did they differ from the vast majority of their race, who never achieved even a moderate level of eco-nomic success and security, but they were constantly made aware that they were not mere duplicates of those whites who did. As they increas-ingly came to recognize, no matter how much economic success they experienced, they would never be accepted as equals by these whites. Further, their level of accomplishment was accentuated by their race. Whites who shared similar levels of economic success never were singled out to the same degree as enterprising blacks.

The second paradox enterprising blacks faced was that even though they experienced their success as individuals, families, and sometimes in groups, often they were viewed as symbolizing the aspirations and prog-ress of their entire race. As a result of this status, and whether they ap-preciated it or not, many of them were forced to live very public lives in which they faced constant scrutiny not only from other blacks but also from whites. Clearly much more was expected of them, in both the private and the public sphere, not simply compared with other blacks but even compared with whites who had achieved similar levels of suc-cess. Although this visibility may have been a source of pride for many, for some it could become a burden. This visibility was summed up in the poem "The Progress of the Race," written by William R. Johnson, of Washington, North Carolina, to celebrate the fiftieth anniversary of general emancipation. The poem was published in the *Star of Zion* on 25 November 1915:

Ever since the Proclamation
  of Emancipation signed,
and the Negro given freedom,
  and been cultured and refined.

He's been making wondrous progress
    keeping up with every race;
and his strong determination
    is to make a better pace.

If you're sick and need a doctor,
    we have Negro doctors too;
and in case you get in trouble,
    at the bar he'll plead for you.

If you want to get salvation,
    and eternal rest to share,
he's a minister, consult him,
    and the Gospel he'll declare.

If you need an education,
    just attend the Negro school;
for he's capable of teaching,
    and enforcing every rule.

If you want a good musician,
    they're accomplished in this art;
for the Negro will assure you,
    he with skill will play his part.

And we have the sweetest singers,
    any nation can produce;
you by no means can excel them,
    and to try it is no use.

And if you desire a palmist
    to tell fortunes from your hand,
he'll impart the information,
    from the Negro palmist stand.

In boxing match he's right there,
    as a pugilist tonight,
and controls the moving pictures,
    oh the Negro he's a sight.

In the nation's best theatres,
    as an actor on the stage,
and as actresses you'll find them
    in the twentieth century age.

We have Negro banks and bankers,
    this is something to relate;
for the progress of the Negro
    is becoming good and great.

And don't mention secret orders,
    they are numerous in the land;
if it's private or fraternal,
    he is leader of the band.

In the great wars of the country
    Negro soldiers with the guns,
stood to fight with courage boldly
    with no cowardice to run.

And he's been a politician,
    and he served his country well;
for in honor and distinction,
    he has been considered swell.

You just can't deny his progress
    in a half of century made;
for the Negro, he is coming,
    and you needn't be afraid.

He is making every effort,
    to ascend the mountain heights;
and he'll reach his destination,
    for in progress he delights.

Appendix

Notes

Selected Bibliography

Index

Appendix
The 5-County Tax List Sample

BEAUFORT, Cabarrus, Caswell, Johnston, and Pasquotank were included in this sample for four reasons related to their geographic and demographic structure as well as their tax lists. First, since their boundaries remained constant during the late nineteenth and the early twentieth century, any changes that occurred in black landholding patterns were not the result of a change in their physical size. Second, geographically they are fairly representative of the location and distribution of the state's black population from 1865 to 1915. Johnston is located in the west central, Beaufort in the east central, and Pasquotank in the northeast part of the coastal plain, the region of the state in which the majority of the state's black population resided. Cabarrus and Caswell are located about 70 miles apart in the piedmont. Further, although the black share of the population in these five counties was three to five percentage points above the statewide average, as with the black population statewide, the percentage steadily declined throughout this period. Whereas the statewide average fell from 36.6 percent in 1870 to 31.6 percent in 1910, the percentage in the 5-county sample declined from 41.2 percent to 34.8 percent. Third, each of the five counties contained both a rural and an urban black population, providing us an opportunity to look at blacks who owned land in the countryside as well as those who owned land in towns. Fourth, and most important, the counties kept tax lists from 1875 to 1895 in fairly consistent 5-year intervals. In every case when a tax list for a given year in the 1875, 1880, 1885, 1890, 1895 sequence had not been preserved or was incomplete, it was possible to find a list for that county from the previous or following year. As indicated by an analysis of Johnston and Pasquotank lists for consecutive years during the early 1880s, there was so little change in a 1-year period that using lists for a county that varied by only one year from the 5-year interval sequence would not significantly alter any measurements. For the sake of literary quality, however, all measurements are expressed in reference to the 5-year-interval sequence.

It is essential to recognize that the format of the county tax lists changed during this period. During the 1870s and the 1880s the race of landowners could only be determined if they paid the poll tax, which was assessed on all men between age 21 and 49. The tax assessor was required to distinguish in each case whether the poll tax was on a black or a white man and to denote the poll's age on the list. Hence, although it is possible to determine the percentage of black polls who owned land and what share of all real estate they owned in their county, black male landowners younger than 21 and older than 49 as well as female landowners are excluded. Beginning in the 1890s, when a new column was included on the tax lists indicating whether a property owner was white or black, it became possible to calculate the share of real estate all black landowners possessed in each county.

Despite the undercounting of black-owned real estate in the pre-1890 tax lists, the 1875, 1880, and 1885 tax lists can be adjusted to gain a better sense of the total real estate owned by all blacks, and not just black polls. By calculating black polls' share of the percentage and value of town lots and acreage owned by all blacks in 1890 (which varied between about one-fourth and one-third), the pre-1890 amounts can be increased proportionately. Before this adjustment there is a false sense that there was as much as a threefold increase in real-estate ownership by blacks between 1885 and 1890. However, as shown in tables 4 and 5, after the adjustment a more predictable shift in landowning patterns emerges.

By 1900, however, the format of tax lists had changed once again. Since some of the counties in the sample were slow to adopt the new format, it was impossible to continue using the tax lists to trace black land acquisition in the 5-county sample. However, soon thereafter the annual *Report of the North Carolina Corporation Commission as a Board of State Tax Commissioners* began to include the total amount of urban and rural real estate owned by blacks in each county of the state. Although these records do not specify the distribution of acreage, note the percentage of black polls who owned land, or allow an analysis of the holdings of specific individuals, they do provide a means to measure the share of real-estate assets blacks owned.

Notes

ABBREVIATIONS

BTWP   Booker T. Washington Papers, The Library of Congress, Washington DC

CFM   Cape Fear Museum, Wilmington NC

DNCB   William S. Powell, ed., *Dictionary of North Carolina Biography*

NCDAH   North Carolina Division of Archives and History, Raleigh

R. G. Dun & Co. Collection   R. G. Dun & Co. Collection, Baker Library, Harvard University Graduate School of Business Administration, Boston

SHC   Southern Historical Collection, Library of the University of North Carolina at Chapel Hill

INTRODUCTION

1. The following sketch of George Allen Mebane is based on my entry "George Allen Mebane," *DNCB* 4:246.

2. I am indebted to Armstead L. Robinson for the term "freedom generation," which he used in "A 'New Birth of Freedom.'"

3. Washington, *The Negro in Business*.

4. Du Bois, *The Negro in Business*. For Du Bois's concern about the impact of slavery on black families, see Du Bois, *The Negro American Family*.

5. Frazier, *The Negro Family*.

6. Elkins, *Slavery*. Elkins's study of slavery and that by the other major historian of slavery in the 1950s, Kenneth Stampp's *Peculiar Institution*, clearly reflect Frazier's emphasis on the deleterious impact of slavery. Prior to the Moynihan Report, Frazier's views on the heritage of slavery and discrimina-

tion, along with those of the black psychologist Kenneth Clark, also influenced the *Brown* v. *Board of Education* decision of 1954.

7. Blassingame, *The Slave Community;* Genovese, *Roll Jordan Roll;* Fogel and Engerman, *Time on the Cross;* Gutman, *The Black Family.*

8. Kolchin, "American Historians," 92.

9. Informative summaries of these studies, which include works by Robert Higgs, Joseph D. Reid Jr., Stephen J. DeCanio, Roger Ransom and Richard Sutch, Gavin Wright, Jay R. Mandle, Jonathan M. Weiner, and Gerald David Jaynes, are found in Woodman, "Sequel to Slavery"; and idem, "Economic Reconstruction." For two studies that point to significant property gains by southern blacks during the decades following the war, see Higgs, "Accumulation of Property by Southern Blacks before World War I"; idem, "Accumulation of Property by Southern Blacks before World War I: Reply"; and Margo, "Accumulation of Property by Southern Blacks before World War I: Comment and Further Evidence."

10. The best study of North Carolina's second reconstruction remains Edmonds, *The Negro and Fusion Politics.*

1. BLACK LANDOWNERSHIP

1. Warren County Deed Book 32:357, NCDAH.

2. The following discussion of Williams's life is based upon Montgomery, *Sketches of Old Warrenton,* 309–10; and North Carolina vol. 24:220, 223, R. G. Dun & Co. Collection. Because the credit ratings use abbreviations and codes, all ratings have been rewritten to improve their literary presentation.

3. Warren County Deed Book 32:378.

4. Ibid., 544.

5. Ibid., 757–58.

6. Ibid., 514–18.

7. Ibid., 444.

8. An examination of the deeds for 21 other counties reveals only a scattering of references to black land recipients or grantees from 1865 to 1870. The 21 other counties are Anson, Buncombe, Camden, Caswell, Chatham, Chowan, Craven, Cumberland, Edgecombe, Franklin, Gaston, Halifax, Lincoln, Martin, Montgomery, Orange, Person, Wake, Wayne, Wilkes, and Wilson. Besides in Warren, the grantee's race sometimes was specified on deeds in Anson, Caswell, Chowan, Cumberland, Edgecombe, Halifax, Orange, and Wake.

9. Chowan County Deed Book R:227, 288.

10. Caswell County Deed Book JJ:431.

11. The deed books for Halifax County covering the period June 1865 through June 1870 contain 1,547 pages. A typical deed takes up two pages. Hence, the lack of any deeds specifying race was not the result of the absence of deeds in the county during this period.

The omission of these black landowners in the deeds raises a number of interesting questions about the process by which blacks gained property. In North Carolina, as in most states at this time, there was no law requiring that deeds be registered. Further, there is little reason to suspect that blacks failed to register their deeds because of racial discrimination. When a black purchased land from a white, it was to the advantage of that white to ensure that the deed was registered in order to prove the transfer of ownership and avoid having to pay property taxes on the land. It is possible that deeds were not registered because the blacks who were buying land were not paying the complete purchase price at the time of the sale but were taking possession of the land by signing a note or mortgage. While generally deeds were not registered until the mortgage was paid off, the blacks would have to pay property taxes in the interim. However, this pattern is difficult to document because counties in North Carolina did not keep separate mortgage records during this era. If blacks were in fact gaining possession of land by using mortgages, this would indicate a willingness on the part of southern whites to extend to blacks a degree of economic trust that historians have not recognized.

12. For the most thorough study of black landownership in the antebellum South, see Schweninger, *Black Property Owners,* esp. chapters 3–5. Schweninger calculates a higher mean value of black-owned real estate in 1860 than I do because whereas I include all black landowners, his sample only includes blacks who owned at least $100 worth of real or personal property. Further, Schweninger includes women in his sample. Despite the variance in our methodology, we identify an identical pattern of average real-estate values falling from 1860 to 1870; Schweninger calculates a 23.5% decline, and I determine the decline to be 22.2%. See Schweninger, *Black Property Owners,* 158.

13. According to Joseph Sitterson's classification for the state's regions, in 1860 the percentage of free black male household heads who owned land was 22.0% in the mountains, 21.5% in the piedmont, and 25.1% in the coastal plain. For the counties included in each region, see Sitterson, *The Secession Movement in North Carolina,* 4–5.

14. Franklin, *The Free Negro in North Carolina,* 18–19, 147.

15. Of the 893 black landowners, 381 (42.7%) made their living outside of agriculture in 1860.

16. Of the 66 black landowners in Craven County, 42 (63.6%) lived in New Bern or resided outside of the town but also had nonagricultural occupations. These 42 owned $12,165 (54.3%) of the $22,415 in land owned by blacks in the county.

17. Of the 43 black landowners in Granville, 22 (51.2%) had nonagricultural occupations.

18. Of the 254 landowners of 1870 classified as black who were found in 1860, 124 (48.8) were enumerated as mulattoes. By contrast, of the 418 mulatto landowners in 1870, only 26 (8.6%) had been listed as black a decade

earlier. This pattern of enumeration suggests not only that there was a significant undercounting of mulattoes in 1870 but that many of the black landowners in 1870 really may have been mulattoes. Hence, the likelihood of mulattoes' owning any real estate in 1870 is probably even greater than is shown in table 1. This finding would seem to indicate that census takers did not enumerate African Americans as mulatto in 1870 just because they owned real estate. This observation may also explain why the percentage of blacks who owned real estate in 1870 was not found to be even further below the 1860 level since more than 90% of the blacks had recently been freed. Hershberg and Williams point to the pattern of census takers' altering their descriptions of skin color in "Mulattoes and Blacks," 396–98.

This tendency of the census takers to underenumerate mulattoes in 1870 may account for Loren Schweninger's conclusion that an increase since 1860 in the percentage of landowners in the Upper South who were black indicates that many of those who were landowners in 1870 had been slaves in 1860. It should be emphasized that Schweninger believes that only one-fifth of the Upper South landowners of 1870 had been free in 1860 (see Schweninger, *Black Property Owners,* 160, 199). Schweninger's estimate of the percentage of 1870 landowners who had been free in 1860 is fairly close to my own.

As for why mulattoes did not experience a sharper decline in landownership, especially since many mulatto landowners were listed as being black, one can speculate that the treatment of enslaved mulattoes may have been better than that of enslaved blacks. After all, half of the mulattoes were free in 1860, compared with fewer than 3% of the blacks. Although the nature of this preferential treatment is difficult to determine, its impact can be measured in terms of their likelihood to gain valuable skills. For example, in 1870 in Orange County, although mulattoes constituted 25.5% of African-American men, they represented 47.9% of the skilled blue-collar workers. These skills, learned under slavery, as well as access to such other forms of favorable treatment as literacy, may have permitted mulattoes after emancipation to accumulate the money necessary to buy real estate. Further, if whites did discriminate against African Americans when selling real estate, as some scholars have argued, the discrimination against mulattoes may have been less severe. For a discussion of the patterns in Orange County, see Kenzer, *Kinship and Neighborhood,* 105, 220–21. Ira Berlin points to mulatto slaves' receiving favorable treatment in *Slaves without Masters,* 151.

19. For evidence that blacks in postwar North Carolina often changed their names, see Alexander, *North Carolina Faces the Freedmen,* 59, 62, 65–6.

20. The percentage of black landowners in 1870 who could be identified as free in 1860 is directly related to their age in 1870: of those less than 20 years, 0% were found; 20–29 years, 11.2%; 30–39 years, 12.7%; 40–49 years, 16.6%; 50–59 years, 20.0%; 60–69 years, 22.0%; 70 years or over, 29.6%. The overall rate was 17.0%.

21. For a discussion of Williams's prewar emancipation, see Montgomery, *Sketches of Old Warrenton,* 309–10.

22. Despite all the problems in linking the 1870 and 1860 censuses, I have been able to identify 676 (17%) of the 3,969 who were landowners in 1870 as having been free in 1860. Again the problem of geographic mobility markedly lowers the likelihood of identifying a greater proportion. Assuming that about one-third of blacks who were free in 1860 remained in the same county until 1870 (a rate I have calculated for Orange County, where 18 of 56 male black household heads, 32.1%, remained during the 1860s), it would be possible to find only 1,323 of 3,969. Therefore, at least half of the 1870 black landowners may have been antebellum freedmen.

23. That these black landowners were free before the end of the Civil War is documented by the 1850 and 1860 manuscript censuses as well as by the Tax Lists of Gates County, 1860, 1861, 1862, microfilm copy in NCDAH.

24. The percentage of mountain blacks owning land was 11.6, compared with 6.0% of the piedmont blacks and 6.8% of the coastal plain blacks. The percentage of mountain blacks who were mulattoes was 15.4, compared with 10.5% of piedmont blacks and 10.2% of coastal plain blacks.

25. Of the 536 black landowners in 1870 who can be identified as freedmen who headed households in 1860, 55.4% owned real estate and 29.5% owned no real estate but did own personal estate. Of the 140 black landowners in 1870 who can be identified as freedmen who were not household heads in 1860, 9.4% owned real estate and 3.6% owned personal estate in their name. Of those 140 nonhousehold heads, 45.0% resided in a household headed by someone with the same surname who owned real estate.

26. Because not all land values were measured in 1870, it is only possible to compare the values of farms for 1860 and 1870. During the 1860s farm values (not including implements and machinery) fell statewide from $143,301,065 to $78,211,083, a decline of 45.4%.

27. These 1,089 men (27.4% of all 3,936) owned real estate valued at $535,726, or 39.1% of all the real estate owned by black male household heads ($1,368,688) in 1870.

28. The success of antebellum free black businessmen in the postwar South is discussed in detail in chapter 2. The restrictions imposed on antebellum free black businessmen and artisans is described in Franklin, *The Free Negro in North Carolina,* 130–39. For an analysis of the occupations of North Carolina soldiers, see Kenzer, *Kinship and Neighborhood,* 176. Schweninger comes to a similar conclusion about the relative success rates of urban blacks and blacks in the countryside in *Black Property Owners,* 147.

29. Forty-nine of the 103 men aged 21 to 44 (47.6%) who owned acreage in 1880 had increased their holdings by 1890; only 23 (22.3%) had suffered a loss. By contrast, only 4 of the 28 men aged 45 to 49 (14.3%) who owned acreage in 1880 had increased their holdings by 1890, and 9 (32.1%) had seen their acreage decrease.

30. In the 5-county sample, 265 of the 3,462 black polls (7.6%) owned land in 1875. By 1895, 665 of the 4,546 black polls (14.6%) were landowners.

31. Because its state government began to collect information on the extent of black landownership soon after the Civil War, Georgia is the one southern state in which it has been thoroughly documented for this era. Three studies that analyze the extent of black ownership of acreage in Georgia are Du Bois, "The Negro Landholder of Georgia"; Banks, "The Economics of Land Tenure in Georgia"; and Raper, *Preface to Peasantry*. In chapter 4 of his study Banks also points to a substantial increase in the number of Georgia blacks who owned fewer than twenty acres during the final three decades of the nineteenth century.

32. Looked at another way, half of the rural landowners owned land valued at less than $100, compared with only a quarter of urban landowners.

33. From 1880 to 1890 black urban landowners experienced a 131.6% increase in their land values, compared with a 71.4% increase for black rural landowners. Twenty-nine black urban landowners experienced an increase in their land values, only 3 experienced a decline, and the land values of 3 remained the same.

34. For biographical information, see "Warren Clay Coleman," *DNCB* 1:401–2.

35. *Wilmington Daily Record*, 28 September 1895.

36. Warren Coleman's holdings were so extraordinary that once they are deleted from the urban landowners' total, their increase becomes 71.4%, compared with 75.5% for the rural landowners.

37. In 1880, 5 of the 358 black polls (1.4%) who were landowners owned both acreage and town lots. By 1890, 16 of the 597 (2.7%) did so. Only 10 of the 172 black polls (5.8%) who owned one form of land in 1880 also owned the other form of land by 1890. Those who owned town lots in 1880 were a bit more likely (3 of 35, or 8.6%) than rural landowners (7 of 137, or 5.1%) to gain ownership of land in the other area by 1890.

Occupation may largely explain why so few men owned both types of land. Although urban land may have been considered a good investment, by making such purchases farmers would only have been limiting the number of rural acres they could buy and put under cultivation. The same is true for urban landowners, who could have more wisely invested their money in either town property or assets related to their trades or professions. In either case, most blacks who had cash seem to have spent it in the real-estate market with which they were most familiar.

38. The best summary of the historical scholarship dealing with whether blacks faced economic discrimination in the postwar South is Woodman, "Sequel to Slavery."

39. From 1905 to 1915 black-owned farm acreage statewide rose from 1,142,726 to 1,444,227, an increase of 301,501 acres, or 26.4%. During the same period white-owned farm acreage increased from 25,334,511 to

25,385,170, an increase of 50,659 acres, or .2%. For information on farm acreage according to race, see *Report of the North Carolina Corporation Commission,* 1906, 1917. Loren Schweninger points to the increase in southern blacks' owner-operated-farm wealth compared with that of whites from 1900 to 1910 in *Black Property Owners,* 183–84.

40. For an analysis of the black urban and rural population by age and sex as well as data on homeownership, see U.S. Bureau of the Census, *Population 1910,* 1:1308–12, 3:290; idem, *Report of the Farms and Homes,* 405. The 1910 published census combined blacks, Indians, Chinese, and Japanese into the category "Colored" when analyzing homeownership. However, since in 1910 the black population in North Carolina dominated this category, counting those in the "Colored" category as blacks does not result in a significant overestimation of the extent of black homeownership statewide. In 1910, 115,975 of 697,843 blacks (16.6%) were classified as urban residents. A small number of these blacks lived in towns and villages with populations under 2,500. Blacks owned 19,627 nonfarm homes and 20,491 farm homes.

For an examination of black homeownership in each of the states in the Upper South for 1870, 1890, and 1910, see Schweninger, *Black Property Owners,* 180.

41. For a detailed description of Clarence Poe's advocacy of rural-land segregation in North Carolina, see Crow, "An Apartheid for the South."

42. *Star of Zion,* 25 February 1915.

43. The following account of the McGhee family is drawn from White, *In Search of Kith and Kin.* White, a McGhee by birth, has compiled the most thorough and best documented history of a North Carolina black family. Her study was supplemented by an examination of the McGhees' property in the Tax Lists of Granville County, 1867–1915, on microfilm in NCDAH.

44. This description of Isaac Forbes is based upon the *Bernian,* 3 November 1877; the *Wilmington Post,* 18 September 1881; and manuscript census, Craven County, 1870, 1880, schedule 4.

45. This account of Ashley W. Smith is drawn from the Ashley W. Smith File, The Public Library of Johnston County and Smithfield, North Carolina. The file contains newspaper clippings and census extracts.

46. Isaac Smith File, provided to me by Stephen E. Massengill, of the North Carolina State Archives. This file is based on Massengill's extensive primary research, including interviews with Smith's descendants. See also Massengill's biographical account of Smith in *DNCB* 5:378–79.

2. THE BLACK BUSINESS COMMUNITY

1. The following description of Alfred Hargrave's career is drawn largely from the Garnett Douglass Hargrave Jr. Interview, Hargrave Family File, CFM.

2. Nearly everything known about southern black businessmen during

the nineteenth century is based on the few biographical accounts of those rare black entrepreneurs who left either autobiographies or personal papers. Among these works are Walker, *Free Frank;* Schweninger, *From Tennessee Slave to St. Louis Entrepreneur;* and Johnson and Roark, *Black Masters.*

A number of examinations of the black business community have revealed important aspects of the circumstances under which southern black entrepreneurs functioned. These include Du Bois, *The Negro in Business;* Washington, *The Negro in Business;* Harmon, "The Negro as a Local Businessman"; and Harris, *The Negro as Capitalist.* In addition to these works, which focus specifically on the black businessman, studies that discuss this topic in either a much more general or a specific context include Meier, *Negro Thought in America,* 126–35; Savage, *Blacks in the West,* 129–35; Weare, *Black Business in the New South;* Wier and Marszalek, *A Black Businessman;* Higgs, *Competition and Coercion;* and Higgs, "Participation of Blacks and Immigrants."

In examining significant numbers of southern black businessmen most scholars have been able to use only business and city directories. See, for example, Blassingame, *Black New Orleans;* Curry, *The Free Black in Urban America;* and Rabinowitz, *Race Relations in the Urban South.* However, since these directories were not always published annually, especially in the South, and because they provide a rather limited amount of information and usually only for the largest cities, they are of limited value for analyzing business patterns.

A number of studies of southern black businessmen have also used the federal published and manuscript census. These studies include, among others, Engerrand, "Black and Mulatto Mobility and Stability"; Hopkins, "Occupational and Geographic Mobility"; and Worthman, "Working Class Mobility." The federal manuscript and published censuses are only marginally beneficial since they identify those blacks who practiced nonagricultural pursuits but do not enumerate whether these blacks actually owned businesses or simply applied their skills and trades in the service of either a white or a black employer. Further, by providing only a snapshot of such individuals once every ten years, the census reveals little about how businesses functioned over a shorter span of time.

3. The best description of the system of credit rating and R. G. Dun & Co. in the mid to late nineteenth century is Norris, *R. G. Dun & Co.* One historical study of North Carolina that also used the R. G. Dun & Co. credit-rating information is Logan, "The Economic Status of the Town Negro in Post-Reconstruction North Carolina." However, Logan used not the actual manuscript ratings but R. G. Dun & Co.'s published quarterly reports, the *Mercantile Agency Reference Book.* This source lists only the name, location, and type of firm, with a coded estimate of net worth and credit status. For another version of Logan's findings, see Logan, *The Negro in North Carolina,* esp. 112–16.

One study that used the R. G. Dun & Co. credit-rating ledgers to study black businessmen in the antebellum South is Walker, "Racism, Slavery, and Free Enterprise." Walker's very valuable examination is not confined to the South and does not use the credit-rating ledgers to trace all of the black businessmen in a state. See also Kenzer, "The Black Business Community in Post Civil War Virginia," "Black Businessmen in Post–Civil War Tennessee," and "Credit Ratings of Georgia Black Businessmen."

There are 25 volumes of credit-rating ledgers for North Carolina, each containing information on approximately eight hundred to one thousand enterprises, hence a total of about 20,000 business ratings. It is a painstaking task to identify black businesses in the credit ledgers since the ratings of blacks were mixed in with those of whites. Fortunately, if a particular businessman was black, the designation "col'd" normally was noted after his name on the credit-ledger page. However, because this designation was not always made, in order to find every black businessman one must read the initial rating citation of each firm, where the businessman's race is always specified.

From the nearly 20,000 North Carolina ratings, 139 black firms can be identified for the years 1841 to 1880. Since the ratings were interrupted in the Confederate states during the four years of the Civil War, they reveal nothing about that period. It was necessary to eliminate 13 of the 139 firms in this analysis as two were conducted only before the war, four were run by women who may have experienced surname changes as a result of marriage, and seven that were initially cited as being located in a North Carolina community were later discovered to never actually have existed in the state.

For the post-1880 period, when the manuscript ledgers ceased, volumes of R. G. Dun & Co.'s *Mercantile Agency Reference Book,* which are housed in the Library of Congress, were used to trace the course of black enterprise in North Carolina. Except for 1895, for which no volume exists in the Library of Congress, it was possible to examine black businesses in 5-year intervals between 1880 and 1905. By 1910, however, this source stopped the practice of specifying the race of businessmen.

For one study of black enterprise in North Carolina during this era that ' does not depend on credit ratings and emphasizes the role of household production as a means to acquire capital, see Holt, "Making Freedom Pay," as well as her larger examination of black economic activity in Granville County, North Carolina, "A Time to Plant."

4. For the credit ratings of Alford, Hargrave, and Jones, see North Carolina vols. 14:18D–18E, 18:277, and 12:557-[8], R. G. Dun & Co. Collection.

5. Of the 126 black credit-rated firms, 16 (12.7%) were located west of Raleigh.

6. Only the post office, not the exact location, of each business is indi-

cated in the credit rating. Further, some black firms may have been located just beyond the incorporated limits of the villages, towns, and cities. If a firm was located particularly far from a community, the credit rating usually stated that, since the site would influence the establishment's success. Few such cases were noted.

The average black population of counties having at least one black firm was 47.7% of the total population in 1870. The statewide black average was 36.6%. Those counties without any black firms had an average black population of 27.1%. Those villages, towns, and cities with at least one black firm had an average black population of 54.7%.

7. No business records of North Carolina black firms for this era have been preserved in the four major depositories in North Carolina—the Special Collections Library of Duke University, the Southern Historical Collection, the East Carolina University Archives, and the North Carolina State Archives.

8. This claim is based on an examination of statewide business directories from this era.

9. Beveridge, *Beveridge and Co.'s North Carolina State Directory,* 405. Lowrey's credit rating can be found in North Carolina vol. 18:186, 203, R. G. Dun & Co. Collection.

10. Of the 126 firms, 104 (82.5%) were proprietorships with a single owner. Of the remaining firms, 12 (9.5%) were 2-member partnerships, 7 (5.6%) were proprietorships that also had the word *company* in their titles, 2 were proprietorships composed of relatives, and 1 (.8%) had multiple partners. For the credit ratings of the firms operated by relatives, see North Carolina vols. 5:248, 257, and 9:498, R. G. Dun & Co. Collection.

11. North Carolina vol. 17:242, ibid.

12. North Carolina vol. 24:213, ibid.; Wellman, *The County of Warren,* 25, 154.

13. A total of 56.1% of the black businessmen described in the credit ledgers and identified in the 1860, 1870, or 1880 manuscript census were mulattoes. The 66 businessmen in this profile conducted 64 of the 126 firms. If a businessman was enumerated as a mulatto in the 1860, 1870, or 1880 manuscript census, he was designated as such in the analysis in table 13. Based on the 1870 manuscript census alone, 30 of the 53 businessmen (56.6%) were mulattoes.

Making positive identifications of all the businessmen in the manuscript census was difficult for two reasons. First, often there were two men having the same name in the same location, often a father-son combination. Second, because few of the businessmen were conducting their businesses as early as 1870 and many were out of business by 1880, it was difficult to link the information found in the census about them directly to the type of business they conducted. If a positive identification between name and type of firm could not be made, the individual was not included in tables 13 and 14.

Edward Byron Reuter pointed to a similar mulatto dominance of the African-American business community in *The Mulatto in the United States,* esp. 293–307. A study that describes the recent literature on mulatto history is Morton, "From Invisible Man to 'New People.'"

14. Determining the exact number of postbellum men who ran businesses and who were free in 1860 is difficult for reasons explained in chapter 1, where the problems of tracing postbellum landowners before the war is described. I have been able to identify only six postbellum businessmen in the 1860 manuscript census. However, community histories indicate that many more blacks were free in 1860 than were recorded in the census. For example, John Hyman, a leading merchant and politician in Warren County, was a free mulatto in 1860, but he was not found in the 1860 manuscript census for Warren County. For Hyman's antebellum status, see Montgomery, *Sketches of Old Warrenton,* 154.

15. The total estate value of the five free blacks who could be identified in both the 1860 and the 1870 manuscript census and who ran both antebellum and postbellum businesses increased during the decade from $1,585 to $11,300, a remarkable increase given the severe decline in property values in the South as well as in North Carolina during this period.

For the credit ratings of Mayzek and Leary, see North Carolina vols. 14: 127 and 6:340, 413, R. G. Dun & Co. Collection.

16. Of the businessmen whose race can be identified from the manuscript census who, according to the credit ledgers, initiated their firms between 1870 and 1880, 25 were mulatto and 27 were black. Of the businessmen whose race can be identified, 75.9% of the blacks could read, compared with 83.8% of the mulattoes.

17. A total of 30 of the 36 (83.3%) mulatto and 24 of the 29 (82.8%) black firms were proprietorships. A total of 13.8% of the blacks formed 2-member partnerships, compared with 5.5% of the mulattoes.

18. From 1876 to 1880 the median age for new entrants was 41 years, much closer to the pre-1873 situation.

19. Ransom and Sutch, *One Kind of Freedom,* esp. chapter 7.

20. North Carolina vol. 18:166I, 186-[9], 186mm, R. G. Dun & Co. Collection.

21. North Carolina vol. 24:217, 220, 223, ibid. Williams's remarkable achievements are documented in chapter 1, above.

22. The quarterly manuscript credit-rating reports end about 1880; thereafter the *Mercantile Agency Reference Book* can be used to trace black firms. After 1905 the *Mercantile Agency Reference Book* stopped denoting race after the names of firms. Although it was possible to trace the 1905 black firms forward to see if they persisted until 1910, it was impossible to determine the number of black firms thereafter.

23. The 1880s is the only decade for which there is at least one surviving quarterly volume of the *Mercantile Agency Reference Book* for each year in the

Library of Congress. Every black firm noted in the January volume for each year in the decade was analyzed, revealing a total of 507 firms: 84 already existing in 1880, of which 17 persisted until 1890; 423 new firms, of which 307 had ceased operating by 1890; and 200 firms in existence in 1890. Of course, because a number of firms may not even have survived for one full year, they would not appear among the 507 because they never were noted in the January volume for any year. For the last three quarters of 1882, a year for which all four volumes exist, 4 firms are listed that did not survive until January 1883. If 1882 was a typical year, therefore, there may have been as many as 40 additional firms in business during the decade, and the failure rate may have been a bit higher than it appears.

24. In *One Kind of Freedom*, 138, Ransom and Sutch note that 63.5% of white rural general stores had a pecuniary strength of at least $2,000 in 1880. The comparable level for all types of black firms in North Carolina was 6.0% in 1880, 3.5% in 1890, and 3.1% in 1900. Another measure of the under-capitalization of blacks firms, as well as the financial direction in which they were heading, was the share of those firms that had less than $500 in pecuniary strength: 71.8% in 1890 and 91.6% in 1900.

25. The racial composition of every community with a black firm cannot be determined for 1890 and 1900 because the published census of 1890 did not enumerate the racial composition of communities smaller than counties and the 1900 census only enumerated racial composition for communities that had more than 2,500 inhabitants.

26. Although 25.0% of the black firms persisted from 1880 to 1885, only 18.5% did so from 1885 to 1890.

27. During the 1890s there was only an 18.6% increase in the number of black firms in the coastal plain, compared with a 110.8% increase in the piedmont.

28. During the 1890s the black population of the piedmont increased by 17.1%, compared with only an 8.2% increase in the coastal plain.

29. Between 1900 and 1910 the black population of the piedmont rose from 212,553 to 229,020, or 7.7%. During the same years the black population of the coastal plain grew from 386,984 to 443,995, or 14.7%.

30. Although the black populations in these two counties were 18.8% and 17.1%, respectively, they stood well above the regional average of 9.1%.

31. By 1900 4,724 of Asheville's 14,694 inhabitants (32.1%) were black.

32. In 1880 there were 32 general stores and 10 groceries. By 1905 there were 90 general stores and 136 groceries.

33. For a discussion of the black Good Templars, see *Star of Zion*, 26 May 1887, 22 May 1897. The prohibition movement in North Carolina is traced in Powell, *North Carolina through Four Centuries*, 451–52.

34. Eleven of the 13 (84.6%) female firms were located in the coastal plain, and 2 were in the piedmont.

35. One of the four businesswomen remained active from 1890 to 1900,

and four of the six remained active from 1900 to 1905. From 1900 to 1905 66.7% of the women remaining active, compared with 44.7% of the men.

36. For a discussion of black businesswomen in the entire South during the antebellum era, see Schweninger, *Black Property Owners,* 85–86.

37. Between 1880 and 1905 the portion of black firms that were not single proprietorships only shifted from 18.1% to 17.4%.

38. The portion of black mercantile firms that were not single proprietorships declined from 29.5% in 1880 to 16.1% in 1905.

39. The following description of York Garrett's business career is derived largely from an interview by the author with Garrett's youngest son, York Garrett Jr., on 16 May 1989 in Durham.

40. York Garrett's involvement in politics is described in Mobley, "In the Shadow of White Society," esp. 356–57, 369.

41. Ibid. Mobley contends that Garrett "moved to more socially prestigious Tarboro after acquiring wealth from his store in Princeville." York Garrett Jr. does not recall his father's operating the store in Princeville, but he would have been only about ten years old when his father moved permanently into Tarboro.

42. *Proceedings of the Most Worshipful Grand Lodge of North Carolina,* 1908 (hereafter cited as *Proceedings of the Grand Lodge*). York Garrett at one time may have been the chief officer of the Mount Lebanon lodge, but this possibility cannot be confirmed in the available records.

43. *Tarboro Southerner,* 10 December 1928, cited in Mobley, "In the Shadow of White Society," 356.

44. During the early twentieth century city directories denoting whether a business was a black firm began to be compiled for a number of North Carolina communities. Table 23 is constructed from 18 directories, for 19 cities, published close to 1915.

45. The only full-length account of the Wilmington race riot is Prather, *We Have Taken a City.*

46. *Sheriff & Cos. Directory of Wilmington, 1875; Directory and General Advertiser of the City of Wilmington for 1894–95; Wilmington, North Carolina Directory,* 1905, 1915.

47. *Durham, North Carolina Directory, 1905–06; Durham, North Carolina Business Directory, 1915–16; Greensboro, North Carolina Directory, 1905–06; Greensboro, North Carolina Business Directory, 1915–16; Walsh's Winston-Salem, North Carolina City Directory for 1904–05; The Winston-Salem, North Carolina City and Suburban Directory, 1915.*

3. COLLECTIVE EFFORTS TOWARD ENTERPRISE

1. The following discussion of Berry O'Kelly is based on "Berry O'Kelly," *DNCB* 4:389–91; R. W. Thompson, "Side Lights," in *Annual Report of the Sixteenth Annual Meeting of the National Negro Business League,* reprint copy in

Box 850, BTWP. I am grateful to Loren Schweninger for providing me with the Berry O'Kelly reference in the BTWP.

2. For a detailed discussion of black Masonry in the United States, see Muraskin, *Middle-Class Blacks in a White Society*. My findings about black Masonry on the state and local level largely support Muraskin's interpretation. For another examination of black Masonry, see Williams, *Black Freemasonry*, 10–20.

3. There is some disagreement about whether the first black Masonic lodge in North Carolina was created in 1865 or 1866. Major S. Hight claims the King Solomon Lodge was created in 1865 in his unpublished account of black Masonry in North Carolina, "Steps of Prince Hall." According to the annual account of the Grand Lodge, *Proceedings of the One Hundred and Seventeenth Annual Communication*, 1987, p. 6, the year was 1866.

4. All subsequent references to the number of members of individual lodges and the state lodge are derived from the 1870, 1880, 1890, 1900, 1908, and 1910 volumes of the *Proceedings of the Grand Lodge*.

5. These 11 members composed 6.1% of the state membership. For lists of black members of the North Carolina legislature, see an inventory compiled by Stephen Massengill, of the North Carolina State Archives (hereinafter cited as Massengill List) and Elaine Nowaczyk's list of black legislators, members of the state constitutional conventions, and those holding county and municipal offices in "The North Carolina Negro in Politics" (hereinafter cited as Nowaczyk List).

6. Twenty-eight of the 50 members (56.0%) of the Giblem Lodge were landowners, and 29 of 54 Masons (53.7%) who were landowners were mulattoes. Information on landownership and color are based on the 1870 manuscript censuses for the counties in which these lodges were located.

7. Only 4 of the 54 members were classified in the 1870 manuscript census as laborers. Four of the Masons also were listed as farmers.

8. Williams, *Black Freemasonry*, 90–91. For a similar perspective on the role of Masonry in general, not just black Masonry, see Doyle, *The Social Order of a Frontier Community*, 182, 185.

9. Credit rating is discussed in chapter 2, above.

10. Twenty-two of the 37 communities (59.4%) with credit-rated black businessmen had black Masonic lodges. In addition to those cases where there was an exact match between a community with a lodge and the presence of a black credit-rated firm, the other 15 communities may also have been linked to credit-rated businessmen; for example, businessmen may have belonged to other lodges in the same county. In addition to the 22 communities with credit-rated black firms and lodges in 1880, 4 other communities with lodges would gain credit-rated black firms by 1885.

11. In addition to its Masonic lodge, there was a black Odd Fellows lodge in Kinston (*Proceedings of the Twenty-Ninth Annual Session of the State Grand Lodge of Odd Fellows*, 1907).

12. This sample of lodges includes the Widow's Sons and the Excelsior Lodges in Raleigh, the Eastern Star Lodge in Elizabeth City, the Doric Lodge in Durham, and the Hiram Lodge in Washington. Information on real-estate ownership was determined from the 1895 tax lists for Pasquotank, Durham, and Beaufort Counties. The percentage of members who owned real estate fell from 34.3% to 25.4%

For a list of Wake County landowners, see Branson, *Farmers and Owners.* Although this source for Wake County is undated, a reading of the source indicates that it was compiled during the 1890s.

Eighty-one of the 236 members (34.3%) of the five lodges in 1890 had owned land in 1895, compared with 65 of the 256 members (25.4%) in 1900. The 1895 tax lists were used in both cases because of problems related to post-1895 tax lists that are noted in the appendix.

13. Thirty-three of the 62 members remained in the Giblem Lodge during the 1890s. In the Doric Lodge only 17 of the 41 members remained during the 1890s.

14. Only 8 of the 25 members (32.0%) of Giblem and Doric in 1900 who had not been members in 1890 owned real estate in 1900. A total of 49 of the 103 members (47.6%) in 1890 owned real estate in 1900.

15. Membership fees are noted in *Proceedings of the Grand Lodge,* 1880, 34.

16. The Mount Moriah Lodge excluded 13 of its 33 members (40.6%) for not paying their dues.

17. Excelsior Lodge Minutes, microfilm copy, NCDAH.

18. Information on the Giblem Lodge is derived from Giblem Lodge Minutes; and from Giblem Lodge Folder, Files on Blacks, CFM. For further discussion of the uses of the Giblem Lodge hall, see Wrenn, *Wilmington,* 193–94.

19. Mount Lebanon Lodge Minutes of Prince Hall Masons, Edgecombe County Memorial Library.

20. The following examples of financial assistance from 1908 are noted in *Proceedings of the Grand Lodge,* 1908, 52–53.

21. Excelsior Lodge Minutes, 26 July 1875.

22. For a demonstration of this custom, see Giblem Lodge Minutes, 10 August 1903, 25 April 1904.

23. Hight, "Steps of Prince Hall." The Hiram Lodge Minutes of 1874, located in the Hiram Prince Hall Masonic Lodge in Washington, North Carolina, provide a detailed assessment list of every member who made a death-benefit contribution; see also *Proceedings of the Grand Lodge,* 1908, 37–40; 1910, 71.

24. *Proceedings of the Grand Lodge,* 1910, 52. For evidence that the individual lodges provided this aid to widows, see Giblem Lodge Minutes, 30 January 1904.

25. Hight, "Steps of Prince Hall"; *Proceedings of the Grand Lodge,* 1910, 59, 71.

26. *Private Laws of North Carolina,* 1879, chapter 120.

27. Logan, "The Colored Industrial Association," 62.

28. See chapter 2, above, for a discussion of Matthew Leary Jr. For information on John S. Leary, see Files on Blacks, CFM.

29. "Ezekiel Ezra Smith," *DNCB* 5:376.

30. Logan, "The Colored Industrial Association," 60.

31. *Raleigh Gazette,* 26 June 1897.

32. Logan, "The Colored Industrial Association," 61.

33. For the various activities of the executive committee, see ibid., 60; *Raleigh Gazette,* 26 September 1885, 31 October 1896; and Logan, *The Negro in North Carolina,* 101–2.

34. *Private Law of North Carolina,* 1897, chapter 218.

35. *Raleigh Gazette,* 4 September 1897.

36. "Lemuel Battle Hinton," in Charles N. Hunter Papers, Special Collections Library, Duke University.

37. See, e.g., the *Raleigh Gazette,* 21 November 1896.

38. In *Charles N. Hunter,* 38, John H. Haley observes that the period of the fair was used for these gatherings, but he provides no specific examples. For an example, see *Raleigh Gazette,* 24 October 1891.

39. *Journal of Industry,* 19 November 1879, clipping in Charles N. Hunter Papers. The speech is also noted in Haley, *Charles N. Hunter,* 49.

40. *Private Laws of North Carolina,* 1868–69, chapters 95, 96, 116, 125, 130, 152; 1870, chapters, 86, 91. I have determined that these institutions were chartered by blacks by examining the names of the members of the board of incorporators.

41. Massengill List.

42. Information on the incorporators of the Warren County Co-operative Business Company has been gathered from the Massengill List, the Nowaczyk List, and the 1870 manuscript census.

43. See above, n. 28.

44. The Registers of the Signatures of the Freedmen's Bank, microfilm copy, NCDAH.

45. On the impact of the failure of the Freedmen's Bank, see Harris, *The Negro as Capitalist,* 25–45.

46. *Star of Zion,* 30 July 1891. For evidence that there may have been branches of the Eastern Building and Loan Association, see ibid., 3 September 1891, 26 February 1892.

47. Ibid., 3 September 1891.

48. Ibid., 27 July 1893.

49. *Raleigh Gazette,* 24 October 1891.

50. *Private Laws of North Carolina,* 1897, chapter 154; *Raleigh Gazette,* 11 September 1897.

51. *Raleigh Gazette,* 12 June, 3 July 1897.

52. Du Bois, *Economic Cooperation,* 138. In *The Negro as Capitalist,* 191–92, Harris indicates that the Mutual Aid Banking Company remained in business until 1914. Although this is surely the case, I have found no North Carolina records to confirm it. According to Harris, the Dime Bank failed in 1903. That same year, Harris notes, another bank, Holloway, Borden, Hicks & Co., was organized in Kinston and remained in business until 1920. Holloway, Borden, Hicks & Co. probably comprised T. B. Holloway, Starr Hicks, and J. L. Borden & Brothers, all of whom were credit-rated black merchants in Kinston.

53. For information on the Forsyth Savings and Trust Company, see *Colored American Magazine* 15 (January 1909): 640; and *Notes on Racial Progress,* 23 January 1909, copy in Box 1094, BTWP.

54. *Private Laws of North Carolina,* 1907, chapter 167.

55. Ibid., 1899, chapter 156. The best study of North Carolina Mutual's formation and development is Weare, *Black Business in the New South.* Because Weare's study is the most thorough examination of any black-controlled North Carolina firm, I will only discuss the insurance company's history as far as it related to the Mechanics and Farmers Bank.

56. The only biography of John Merrick is Andrews, *John Merrick.* A brief background study of Merrick can be found in Meier, *Negro Thought in America,* 144.

57. Booker Taliaferro Washington, "Durham, North Carolina: A City of Negro Enterprises," *Independent* 70 (30 March 1911): 645.

58. For information on Aaron Moore, see Weare, *Black Business in the New South,* 29–30, 34, 36, 45–49, 57; Kennedy, *The North Carolina Mutual Story,* 4–6; and manuscript census, Columbus County, 1870, schedule 1.

59. On their participation in these churches see, *Raleigh News and Observer,* 22 January 1978, clipping in St. Joseph A.M.E.Z. File, Durham County Public Library; "A Historical Sketch of the White Rock Baptist Church," Durham County Library; and Boyd, *The Story of Durham,* 292. Weare provides a thorough discussion of the role of the directors of both firms in these churches in *Black Business in the New South,* 54–55, 87, 189–95, 224. For their involvement in Masonry, see *Proceedings of the Grand Lodge,* 1908, 1910.

60. Boyd, *The Story of Durham,* 286, 289. The bank's resources of $301,239.66 are denoted in North Carolina Corporation Commission, *Reports of the Condition of the State Banks of North Carolina at the Close of Business on December 29, 1920,* 44. In *The Negro as Capitalist,* 193, Harris lists the total resources of black banks in North Carolina as $529,400; hence, the Mechanics and Farmers Bank's share would have been 56.9%.

61. Kennedy, *The North Carolina Mutual Story,* 289.

62. *Report of the Third Annual Convention of the National Negro Business League,* 142, copy in Box 1034, BTWP.

63. *Report of the Ninth Annual Convention of the National Negro Business*

League, 11, copy in ibid. For a discussion of the creation of the state organization, see *Raleigh News and Observer,* 28 October 1909, clipping in Box 847, BTWP.

64. *Report of the Seventeenth Session of the National Negro Business League,* 226–27, copy in Box 857, BTWP.

65. This analysis of the relation between League chapters and communities with credit-rated black firms is based on the 1905 *Mercantile Agency Reference Book,* the last volume of which notes the race of proprietors of credit-rated businesses. There were 116 communities with black credit-rated firms in 1905. The 24 communities (20.7% of all such communities) represented 149 of the 320 (46.5%) credit-rated black firms in 1905.

66. Walter P. Evans to Emmett J. Scott, 23 April 1914, Box 853, BTWP.

67. For a discussion of the $2 membership fee for enrollment in the League, see Samuel H. Vick to Emmett J. Scott, 6 August 1913, Box 849, ibid.

68. *Proceedings of the Grand Lodge,* 1910.

69. *Notes on Racial Progress,* 10 March 1910, copy in Box 1094, BTWP.

70. The following account of Richard Fitzgerald is taken from Murray, *Proud Shoes,* 217, 225, 227, 267; and Washington, "Durham, North Carolina," 644.

71. Thompson, "Side Lights."

72. In *Negro Thought in America,* 127, Meier discusses the role subsidiary societies played in the structure of the National Negro Business League. Walter Weare describes the involvement of the North Carolina Mutual in the League and especially in the affiliate organization, the National Association of Negro Insurance Men, in *Black Business in the New South,* 144–46, 208–09.

4. THE POLITICS OF ENTERPRISE

1. The following accounts of black politicians that make reference to their occupations or the amount of property they owned in either 1860 or 1870 are based on the manuscript census returns for those years in the counties specified in the text. Any references to businesses these politicians conducted are based on information from the *Mercantile Agency Reference Book.* As in chapter 3, the names of black members of the state legislature are derived from the Massengill and Nowaczyk Lists. Additional biographical information on black state assemblymen and senators is drawn from the manuals published on the membership of the legislature, whose various titles include *Legislative Record* (1877), *Tar Heel Sketch-Book* (1879), *Assembly Sketch Book* (1883 and 1885); *Legislative Biographical Sketch Book* (1887); and *State Officers and General Assembly of North Carolina* (1893).

2. African Methodist Episcopal Zion Church, *Quarterly Review* 23 (July–September 1906): 106.

3. There is some difference of opinion about how many blacks served as delegates to the 1868 state constitutional convention. Nowaczyk lists 13 in

"The North Carolina Negro in Politics," but Hamilton claimed there were
15 in his *Reconstruction in North Carolina;* for Hamilton's list of black delegates,
see p. 254. I have chosen to accept Nowaczyk's figure because 2 of the delegates that Hamilton asserted were blacks were never noted in other sources
as being black or as having held any other office.

4. "Confederate Tax Census for Bertie County, North Carolina, 1862,"
Genealogical Services Branch, North Carolina State Library.

5. Montgomery, *Sketches of Old Warrenton,* 154. For Hyman's credit rating,
see North Carolina vol. 24:193, 217, R. G. Dun & Co. Collection.

6. "James Henry Harris," *DNCB* 3:53.

7. "Abraham H. Galloway," ibid., 2:271–72. In 1870 Galloway owned
$25 in real estate in Brunswick County.

8. Ten of the 19 black legislators who served before 1870 (53.6%)
owned real estate in 1870. Of the 70 black members of the legislature who
served between 1868 and 1878, 28 (40.0%) were landowners in 1870. Sixteen of the 28 who served in the legislature from 1868 to 1878 and who
owned land in 1870 (57.1%) were enumerated as mulattoes on the manuscript census. Thomas Holt points to the disproportionate role mulattoes
played in the South Carolina legislature and their voting differences with
blacks in *Black over White,* 59, 126, 162.

9. For a discussion of the Leary Family, see chapters 2 and 3, above.

10. North Carolina vol. 5:248J, R. G. Dun & Co. Collection.

11. Hugh Cale's property is enumerated on the Tax List of Pasquotank
County, 1885, NCDAH.

12. Seventeen of the 71 blacks elected to the legislature before 1880 also
served in the state house or senate during the 1880s and 1890s.

13. In addition to sketches on Williamson in the manuals of the state legislature, there is a valuable account of his career in Penn, *The Afro-American
Press,* 180–83.

14. Of the 15 members of the legislature whose birth year can be determined from the manuals of the legislature who served both before and after
1880, the median year of birth was 1842.

15. The median year of birth of the 29 members of the legislature who
served only after 1880 and whose birth year can be determined was 1854. A
total of 20 were born after 1850, and at least 3 were born after 1865.

16. It is possible to determine the level of education of only 29 of the
52 post-1880 black legislators for whom there is a biographical sketch in the
manuals of the state legislature. Eleven of these sketches note the college
the member attended.

17. "George H. White," *DNCB,* forthcoming.

18. "Henry P. Cheatham," ibid., 1:359–60.

19. *Raleigh News and Observer,* 24 August 1899.

20. "James Hunter Young" *DNCB,* forthcoming; "Stewart Ellison," ibid.,
2:152–53.

21. U.S. Department of Interior, *Official Register of the United States,* 1884, 1:125.

22. Valuable insight on the Howe family both before and after the war can be gained from reading the McDonald Howe Papers, Manuscripts Collection, William Randall Library, University of North Carolina at Wilmington.

23. Hamilton, *Reconstruction in North Carolina,* 646.

24. U.S. Department of Interior, *Official Register of the United States,* 1891, 2:1121.

25. For Howe's attempt to gain the collectorship, see *Star of Zion,* 15 July 1897.

26. I have only been able to identify two of the black members of the legislature as ministers.

27. Although his name appears in the 1887 manual of the state legislature, Hoover is not noted on the Massengill List as a black member of the state house. His firms can be traced in *Mercantile Agency Reference Book,* 1875–1905.

28. Thomas Fuller's attempt to pass a bill to incorporate the North Carolina Mutual and Provident Association is noted in Edmonds, *The Negro and Fusion Politics,* 110–11. Fuller's difficulties are described more fully in Weare, *Black Business in the New South,* 30–32.

29. I have examined every private bill passed by the North Carolina legislature between 1868 and 1915 in order to discover its relation to a black institution. This often can be determined from the title of the bill, but it is usually necessary to read the names of the incorporators. I have identified 76 bills passed from 1868 through 1899 as related to black institutions. Between 1901 and 1915 there were only 6 such bills.

30. *Branson's North Carolina Business Directory* for 1869, 1872, and 1877–78 contains the names of 20 black county commissioners and 21 black town aldermen residing in 17 different counties.

31. Ibid. Thirteen of the 41 local officeholders owned real estate in 1870, and 9 of these 13 were mulattoes.

32. North Carolina vol. 5:246, 248m, R. G. Dun & Co. Collection.

33. The 1870 manuscript census of Edgecombe County enumerates John Dancy Sr. as well as his wife and other children as a black, but Frank is listed as a mulatto. Perhaps Frank, who appears to be the oldest son, had another mother. For a discussion of the Dancy family that does not provide an explanation for this topic, see Dancy, *Sand against the Wind,* 60–71.

34. John Dancy Sr. is noted as a county commissioner in Quick, *Negro Stars,* 172.

35. For the procedure by which Frank Dancy was chosen mayor of Tarboro, see undated document [1898], Marion Butler Papers, SHC.

36. "John Campbell Dancy, Jr.," *DNCB* 2:7–8.

37. North Carolina vol. 18:279, R. G. Dun & Co. Collection.

38. North Carolina vol. 18:186, 203, ibid.

39. North Carolina vol. 6:376, ibid.

40. A total of 27, or 21.4%, of the black credit-rated firms sold liquor during the 1870s. For Johnson's credit rating, see North Carolina vol. 24: 248, ibid.

41. Edmonds, *The Negro and Fusion Politics,* 117–18.

42. Ibid., 67–70.

43. Five out of 11 black firms selling liquor in 1877 went out of business in either 1878 or 1879. For the best discussion of the purpose and results of the 1877 North Carolina County Government Act, see Logan, *The Negro in North Carolina,* 29–30, 49, 50, 54–55, 118–19, 125–26, 218–19.

44. North Carolina vol. 23:438, R. G. Dun & Co. Collection. The net number of firms is calculated by subtracting the number of firms that failed each year from the number of new firms created during that year. Whereas 44 net firms were created between 1865 and 1875, or 4.0 net firms per year, only 5 net firms were created between 1876 and 1878, or 1.67 net firms per year.

45. North Carolina vol. 15:73, ibid. The Jamesville postmastership paid $240.06 in 1875 and $245.33 in 1877. For the amount earned each year, see *Official Register of the United States,* 1875, 2:1,027; 1877, 2:666.

46. According to the *Official Register of the United States* for these years, a number of postmasterships in North Carolina paid more than $2,000 per year, but blacks held none of these.

47. Ibid., 1891, 2:1,017.

48. *Raleigh Gazette,* 14 August 1897.

49. The following account of Samuel H. Vick is drawn from "Samuel H. Vick," in Richardson, *The National Encyclopedia of the Colored Race,* 235; and Anderson, *Race and Politics,* 168, 169, 197n, 245. 246, 250.

50. John E. Woodard to M. W. Ransom, 14 April 1889, Matt Ransom Papers, SHC.

51. *Official Register of the United States,* 1889, 2:954.

52. Anderson, *Race and Politics,* 82, 103–4; *Star of Zion,* 16 April 1886.

53. *Star of Zion,* 15 January 1892.

54. This observation is made in both Edmonds, *The Negro and Fusion Politics,* 117–35, and Anderson, *Race and Politics,* esp. 255.

55. John S. Leary to D. L. Russell, 9 December 1896, Daniel Russell Papers, SHC. Leary noted considering a post in the mint in Charlotte, but he probably meant the federal assay office in that city.

56. R. H. Rick et al. to Marion Butler, 9 April 1898, Marion Butler Papers, SHC.

57. Thos. H. Battle to Marion Butler, 16 April 1898, ibid.

58. W. A. Dunn to Marion Butler, 19 April, 22 July 1898, and R. J. Lewis to Marion Butler, 3 May 1898, ibid.

59. For the number of black registered voters and the North Carolina Republicans' policy of excluding blacks from patronage, see Haley, *Charles N. Hunter,* 154.

60. Eric Anderson provides a list of eleven blacks in the Second Congressional District whose appointments as postmaster were confirmed in 1897 and 1898 in *Race and Politics,* 246. None of these black postmasters retained their office ten years later (*Official Register of the United States,* 1907, 2:365–78).

61. The question whether North Carolina blacks could have improved their economic status at a greater rate if they had not been disfranchised somewhat parallels Thomas Holt's question whether South Carolina blacks could have avoided eventual disfranchisement if they had been able to maintain political unity after 1876 (see Holt, *Black over White,* chapter 9).

5. FAMILY, MARRIAGE, AND EDUCATION

1. This account of John Clarence Scarborough Sr. and J. C. Hargett is based on two press releases, "At Age 94—Pioneer Durham Businessman J. C. Scarborough Succumbs," 30 January 1972, and "Re-Dedication Service 100th Anniversary Founding Scarborough Chapels and Gardens," 26 June 1988, Scarborough Funeral Home Records, Scarborough Funeral Home. For evidence that the two Lowreys were brothers, see *Raleigh Gazette,* 5 June 1897. Note that Scarborough's correct age at death was 93, not 94.

2. The strong consideration of Hargett for the postmastership of Kinston is noted in *Raleigh Gazette,* 1 May 1897.

3. The most thorough discussion of marriage under slavery can be found in Gutman, *The Black Family.*

4. On North Carolina free blacks marrying slaves, see Franklin, *The Free Negro in North Carolina,* 185. As evidence that in 1860 most free black men were not married to slave women, I was only able to classify 507 out of 3,680 free men who headed households (13.8%) as either single or widowers based on the age and name of the women listed after them on the manuscript census. Although in fact some of these men may have been married to slave women, whose name would not have appeared on the schedule of free inhabitants, this was probably rarely the case. By 1870 only 9.2% of the men who headed households were single or widowers. If many free black men had had slave wives in 1860, there would have been a much more dramatic decline in these percentages between 1860 and 1870.

5. Another study that discusses the intermarriage of blacks and mulattoes and points to the differences in property ownership based upon color is Hershberg and Williams, "Mulattoes and Blacks."

6. Ross and King, *Marriage Register of Johnston County.* Ross and King's compilation of 137 black marriages sometimes includes the names of the parents of the bride and groom as well as the ages of the bride and groom.

Using this information to examine all of the 1870 black households in Johnston County, I identified 32 marriages in which the groom's parents owned real estate. In order to discover whether the parents of any of these grooms owned real estate outside of Johnston County, I examined all of the households in the seven counties immediately bordering Johnston: Franklin, Wake, Harnett, Sampson, Wayne, Wilson, and Nash. The parents of none of these grooms owned real estate in any of these other counties.

7. In 13 of the 32 marriages the parents of the groom owned less than $100 in real estate.

8. Information on real-estate ownership after 1870 is based on the Johnston County tax scrolls for the years specified in the text.

9. *Star of Zion*, 12 January 1898. For the best examination of black upper-class club life nationally, see Gatewood, *Aristocrats of Color*, 210–46. Janette Thomas Greenwood provides an outstanding description of the black upper class of Charlotte in *Bittersweet Legacy*. Although Greenwood and I both discuss black social life in Charlotte, few of our specific examples overlap.

10. *Annual Catalogue of the Leonard Medical School*, 1912.

11. *Star of Zion*, 30 March 1899.

12. Ibid., 18 February 1915.

13. *Star of Zion*, 16 January 1902.

14. Ibid., 23 January 1902, 11 February 1904. Gatewood provides an insightful look at black literary societies in *Aristocrats of Color*, 213–24.

15. Ibid., 19 August 1909.

16. Ibid., 28 January 1915.

17. Ibid., 15 July 1915.

18. For basic chronologies of black colleges in North Carolina, see Brown, *A History of the Education of Negroes;* and Powell, *Higher Education.*

19. U.S. Commissioner of Education, *Report of the Commissioner of Education for the Year 1899–1900*, 2:2518–19. This report failed to include the graduates of Biddle College for that year; fortunately, this number was recorded in Du Bois and Dill, *The College-Bred Negro American*, 50–51. Fifty-one of the 58 college graduates during the 1899–1900 academic year received bachelor's degrees from the seven denominational colleges, and 7 graduated from North Carolina A&M.

20. The following discussion of black college students is based on an examination of the various college catalogues of these institutions, many of which are housed in the North Carolina Collection at the Library of the University of North Carolina. In most cases these catalogues list the names and hometowns of the students in attendance. Further, the catalogues note the names of all of the alumni, where these alumni were living, and their present occupations.

In analyzing the locations of the hometowns of these students in relation to that of the college, it should be noted that some of the students were not

North Carolina residents. This was particularly the case of Biddle students, many of whom were South Carolinians from communities near Charlotte. Livingstone College also tended to attract a fair number of out-of-state students and even some foreign students, especially from Africa and the Caribbean.

21. The similarities in the costs of attending the various colleges and in their academic calendars was determined by an examination of the annual catalogues of the various schools.

22. The best discussion of the relation between normal schools and colleges is found in Anderson, *The Education of Blacks*, 34–35.

23. *Annual Catalogue of Shaw University*, 1882, 26. For a valuable description of curriculum, see ibid., 28–29.

24. *Annual Catalogue of Scotia Seminary*, 1894–95.

25. *Annual Catalogue of Bennett College*, 1914. For the best count of Bennett graduates see, Du Bois and Dill, *The College-Bred Negro American*, 50–51.

26. *Annual Catalogue of Kittrell College*, 1906–7.

27. *Annual Catalogue of Livingstone College*, 1915–16.

28. *Annual Catalogue of Biddle College*, 1919–20. The Biddle College catalogue also indicates that it granted 202 master's degree during these years. However, it does not note what constituted a master's degree. The Biddle College catalogue and Du Bois and Dill's *The College-Bred Negro American* differ on the number of bachelor's degrees granted by Biddle: the former indicates 199, whereas the latter states 275.

29. *Annual Catalogue of St. Augustine's School*, 1917–18.

30. *Annual Catalogue of Biddle College*, 1919–20.

31. For the number of professional degrees granted by Shaw, see Carter, *Shaw's Universe*, 194–95.

32. For an insightful history of the Taylor family and especially the levels of education attained by its members, see Beryl D. Anderson, "Taylor Family History," Taylor Family History, CFM.

33. Based on the manuscript census for the counties in which the undergraduates resided (as noted in the Shaw catalogue), it appears that 14 of the 79 male undergraduates in the college department of Shaw during the 1876–77 and 1878–79 academic years (17.7%) had parents who had owned real estate in 1870.

34. Only 9 of the 40 undergraduate men at Shaw during the 1876–77 academic year eventually received their bachelor's degree from the school. During the 1891–92 academic year 10 of the 31 undergraduate men graduated. At Livingstone during the 1895–96 academic year 8 of the 11 undergraduate men received their degree. And 34 of the 43 Shaw undergraduate men attending Shaw during the 1899–1900, 1900–1901, and 1901–2 academic years eventually graduated.

35. Eight of the 11 junior and senior men at Biddle and Livingstone graduated.

36. *Annual Catalogue of Biddle College,* 1882–83, 22. The average of $70 per teacher was determined by dividing the $5,000 total by 73 students, yielding $68.49 per teacher.

37. The following account of Thomas Fuller is based on his autobiography, *Twenty Years in Public Life,* 10–46. Henderson Fuller's property value can be found in the 1870 manuscript census returns of Franklin County.

38. A total of 297 of the 443 graduates (67.0%) worked in education and/or the clergy.

39. Fifty-eight of the 443 graduates (13.1%) worked in medicine.

40. The Darden family history is contained in Darden and Darden, *Spoonbread and Strawberry Wine.*

41. *Annual Catalogue of the Leonard Medical School,* 1912.

42. Only 15 of the 82 graduates of the Leonard Medical School from 1886 to 1905 (18.3%) returned to practice in their hometowns.

43. Fifty of the 443 graduates in the 4-school sample (11.3%) pursued business careers.

44. Only 6 of the 143 pre-1900 graduates (4.2%) pursued business careers, whereas 44 of the 300 post-1900 graduates (14.7%) did so.

45. Nineteen of the 45 North Carolina Agricultural and Mechanical graduates from 1899 to 1908 (42.2%) pursued business careers. For the occupations followed by these graduates, see *Bulletin of A&T College,* 1917. Another 20 of the 45 graduates (44.4%) went into education. For Donnell and Merrick's employment with North Carolina Mutual and their familial tie, see Weare, *Black Business in the New South,* 91, 110–11, 138–39.

46. William Clement, interview with author, 9 May 1989, Durham.

47. Weare, *Black Business in the New South,* 86–89, 90.

Selected Bibliography

PRIMARY SOURCES

Archive Collections

Baker Library, Harvard University Graduate School of Business Administration, Boston.
    R. G. Dun & Co. Collection. North Carolina vols. 1–25.
Cape Fear Museum, Wilmington NC.
    Beryl D. Anderson. "Taylor Family History." Taylor Family File.
    Giblem Lodge Folder. Files on Blacks.
    Garnett Douglass Hargrave Jr. Interview. Hargrave Family File.
Durham County Public Library, Durham NC.
    "A Historical Sketch of the White Rock Baptist Church."
    St. Joseph A.M.E.Z. File.
Edgecombe County Memorial Library, Tarboro NC.
    Mount Lebanon Lodge Minutes of Prince Hall Masons.
Genealogical Services Branch, North Carolina State Library, Raleigh NC.
    "Confederate Tax Census for Bertie County, North Carolina, 1862." Manuscript compiled by the United States History Class, 1975–76, Rowan Church Academy.
Giblem Lodge, Wilmington NC.
    Giblem Lodge Minutes.
Harold B. Lee Library, Brigham Young University, Provo UT.
    Manuscript Census of the United States, 1850, 1860, 1870, 1880, 1900. North Carolina. Microfilm copy.
Hiram Prince Hall Masonic Lodge, Washington NC.
    Hiram Lodge Minutes of 1874.

Library of Congress, Washington DC.
   National Negro Business League Files. Booker T. Washington Papers.
North Carolina Collection, Library of the University of North Carolina at
   Chapel Hill, Chapel Hill NC.
   Annual Catalogue of Bennett College, 1914.
   Annual Catalogue of Biddle College, 1882–83, 1919–20.
   Annual Catalogue of Kittrell College, 1906–7.
   Annual Catalogue of Livingstone College, 1915–16.
   Annual Catalogue of the Leonard Medical School, 1912.
   Annual Catalogue of Scotia Seminary, 1894–95.
   Annual Catalogue of Shaw University, 1882.
   Annual Catalogue of St. Augustine's School, 1917–18.
   Bulletin of A. & T. College, 1917.
   *Proceedings of the Twenty-Ninth Annual Session of the State Grand Lodge of Odd
   Fellows,* 1907.
North Carolina Division of Archives and History, Manuscripts, Raleigh NC.
   Deed Books of Anson, Buncombe, Camden, Caswell, Chatham, Chowan,
   Cumberland, Edgecombe, Franklin, Gaston, Halifax, Lincoln, Martin,
   Montgomery, Orange, Person, Wake, Warren, Wayne, Wilkes, and Wilson.
   Excelsior Lodge Minutes. Microfilm copy.
   The Registers of the Signatures of the Freedmen's Bank. Microfilm copy.
   Isaac Smith File.
   Tax Lists of Beaufort, Cabarrus, Caswell, Johnston, and Pasquotank Coun-
   ties, 1875, 1880, 1885, 1890, 1895.
   Tax Lists of Gates County, 1860, 1861, 1862.
   Tax List of Granville County, 1867–1915.
The Public Library of Johnston County and Smithfield, North Carolina,
   Smithfield NC.
   Ashley W. Smith File.
Scarborough Funeral Home, Durham NC.
   Scarborough Funeral Home Records.
Southern Historical Collection, Library of the University of North Carolina
   at Chapel Hill, Chapel Hill NC.
   Marion Butler Papers.
   Matt Ransom Papers.
   Daniel Russell Papers.
Special Collections Library, Duke University, Durham NC.
   Charles N. Hunter Papers.
State Grand Lodge Office of Prince Hall Grand Lodge Free and Accepted
   Masons, Durham NC.
   Major S. Hight. "Steps of Prince Hall."
   Proceedings of the Most Worshipful Grand Lodge of North Carolina, 1870, 1880,
   1890, 1900, 1908, 1910.

Proceedings of the One Hundred and Seventeenth Annual Communication, 1987.
Manuscripts Collection, William Randall Library, University of North Carolina at Wilmington, Wilmington NC.
McDonald Howe Papers.

Newspapers

Bernian
Carolina Enterprise
Raleigh Gazette
Raleigh News and Observer
Star of Zion
Wilmington Daily Record
Wilmington Post

Magazines and Periodicals

Colored American Magazine
Independent
Quarterly Review of the African Methodist Episcopal Zion Church

Oral Interviews

William Clement, interview by author, 9 May 1989, Durham NC.
York Garrett Jr., interview by author, 16 May 1989, Durham NC.

Directories
Statewide

Beveridge, William Henry, comp. *Beveridge and Co.'s North Carolina State Directory, 1877–78*. Raleigh: News Publishing Company, n.d.
Branson's North Carolina Business Directory for 1869. Raleigh: J. A. Jones, n.d.
Branson's North Carolina Business Directory for 1872. Raleigh: J. A. Jones, n.d.
Branson's North Carolina Business Directory for 1877 and 1878. Raleigh: L. Branson, n.d.

Directories of Specific Communities (listed alphabetically by community name)

The Asheville, North Carolina, City Directory. Asheville: Piedmont Directory Company, 1916.
Directory of Burlington, Graham and Haw River, North Carolina, 1909–1910. Asheville: Piedmont Directory Company, 1910.
Charlotte, North Carolina City Directory, 1915. Asheville: Piedmont Directory Company, n.d.
Concord, North Carolina City Directory, 1916–17. Asheville: Piedmont Directory Company, n.d.

Durham, North Carolina Directory, 1905–06. Durham: Hill Directory Company, 1905.

Durham, North Carolina Business Directory, 1915–16. Durham: Hill Directory Company, 1915.

Fayetteville, N.C. Directory, 1915–16. Vol. 1. Florence SC: Chas. S. Gardener, 1916.

Gastonia, North Carolina City Directory, 1910–11. Gastonia: Piedmont Directory Company, 1910.

Greensboro, North Carolina Directory, 1905–06. Greensboro: Hill Directory Company, 1905.

Greensboro, North Carolina Business Directory, 1915–16. Greensboro: Hill Directory Company, 1915.

High Point, North Carolina City Directory, 1910–11. High Point: Piedmont Directory Company, 1910.

Official Directory City of New Bern, N.C., 1916–17. Florence SC: Chas. S. Gardener, 1917.

Raleigh, North Carolina City Directory, 1915. Richmond VA: Piedmont Directory Company, 1915.

Rocky Mount, North Carolina Directory, 1912–13. Rocky Mount: Hill Directory Company, 1912.

The Salisbury-Spencer, North Carolina City and Suburban Directory, 1915–16. Asheville: Piedmont Directory Company, 1915.

Statesville, North Carolina City Directory, 1916–17. Statesville: Piedmont Series, 1916.

Branson, Levi, ed. *Farmers and Owners of Land in Wake County.* Raleigh: L. Branson, n.d.

The Washington, North Carolina City Directory, 1916–17. Asheville: Piedmont Press, n.d.

Sheriff & Cos. Directory of Wilmington, 1875. N.p., n.d.

Directory and General Advertiser of the City of Wilmington for 1894–95. Wilmington: H. Gerken, 1895.

Wilmington, North Carolina Directory, 1905. Richmond VA: Hill Directory Company, 1905.

Wilmington, North Carolina Directory, 1915. Wilmington: Hill Directory Company, 1915.

Wilson, North Carolina Directory, 1916–17. Wilson: Hill Directory Company, 1916.

Walsh's Winston-Salem, North Carolina City Directory for 1904–05. Charleston SC: W. H. Walsh Directory Company, 1904.

The Winston-Salem, North Carolina City and Suburban Directory, 1915. Asheville: Piedmont Directory Company, 1915.

Government Documents
Federal

Du Bois, W. E. B. "The Negro Landholder of Georgia." *Bulletin of the Department of Labor* 6 (July 1901): 647–77.
U.S. Bureau of the Census. *The Statistics of the Populations of the United States in June 1, 1870.* Washington DC: GPO, 1873.
————. *Report of the Farms and Homes: Proprietorships and Indebtedness.* Washington DC: GPO, 1896.
————. *Population 1910.* Vols. 1 and 3. Washington DC: GPO, 1913.
U.S. Commissioner of Education. *Report of the Commissioner of Education for the Year 1899–1900.* 2 vols. Washington DC: GPO, 1901.
U.S. Department of Interior. *Official Register of the United States.* Washington DC: GPO, 1877, 1884, 1891, 1907.

State of North Carolina

Legislative Biographical Sketch Book, Session 1887. Raleigh: Edwards, Broughton, 1887.
North Carolina Corporation Commission. *Reports of the Condition of the State Banks of North Carolina at the Close of Business on December 29, 1920.* Raleigh: Edwards & Broughton, 1921.
Private Laws of North Carolina, 1867–1915.
Report of the North Carolina Corporation Commission as a Board of State Tax Commissioners, 1906, 1917.
Shotwell, R. A., and Natt Atkinson. *Legislative Record, Giving the Acts Passed Session Ending May, 1877 Together with Sketches of the Lives and Public Acts of the Members of both Houses.* Raleigh: Edwards, Broughton, 1877.
State Officers and General Assembly of North Carolina, 1893. N.p., n.d.
Tomlinson, J. S. *Assembly Sketch Book.* Raleigh: Edwards, Broughton, 1883, 1885.
————. *Tar Heel Sketch-Book: A Brief Biographical Sketch of the Life and Public Acts of the Members of the General Assembly of North Carolina, Session of 1879.* Raleigh: Raleigh News Steam Book, 1879.

SECONDARY SOURCES
Books

Alexander, Roberta Sue. *North Carolina Faces the Freedmen: Race Relations during Presidential Reconstruction, 1865–1867.* Durham: Duke Univ. Press, 1985.
Anderson, Eric. *Race and Politics in North Carolina, 1872–1901.* Baton Rouge: Louisiana State Univ. Press, 1981.
Anderson, James D. *The Education of Blacks in the South, 1865–1935.* Chapel Hill: Univ. of North Carolina Press, 1988.
Andrews, Robert McCants. *John Merrick, A Biographical Sketch.* Durham: Seeman Printery, 1920.

Ayers, Edward L. *The Promise of the New South: Life after Reconstruction.* New York: Oxford Univ. Press, 1992.

Berlin, Ira. *Slaves without Masters: The Free Negro in the Antebellum South.* New York: Pantheon, 1975.

Blassingame, John W. *Black New Orleans, 1860–1880.* Chicago: Univ. of Chicago Press, 1973.

—————. *The Slave Community: Plantation Life in the Antebellum South.* New York: Oxford Univ. Press, 1972.

Boles, John B., and Evelyn Thomas Nolen. *Interpreting Southern History: Historiographical Essays in Honor of Sanford W. Higginbotham.* Baton Rouge: Louisiana State Univ. Press, 1987.

Boyd, William Kenneth. *The Story of Durham: City of the New South.* Durham: Duke Univ. Press, 1925.

Brown, Hugh Victor. *A History of the Education of Negroes in North Carolina.* Raleigh: Irving-Swain, 1961.

Carter, Wilmoth A. *Shaw's Universe, A Monument to Educational Innovation.* Rockville MD: D.C. National Publishing, 1973.

Curry, Leonard P. *The Free Black in Urban America, 1800–1850: The Shadow of the Dream.* Chicago: Univ. of Chicago Press, 1981.

Dancy, John C. *Sand against the Wind: The Memoirs of John C. Dancy.* Detroit: Wayne State Univ. Press, 1966.

Darden, Norma Jean, and Carole Darden. *Spoonbread and Strawberry Wine: Recipes and Reminiscences of a Family.* Garden City NJ: Anchor, 1978.

Doyle, Don H. *The Social Order of a Frontier Community: Jacksonville, Illinois, 1825–1870.* Urbana: Univ. of Illinois Press, 1978.

Du Bois, W. E. B., ed. *Economic Cooperation among Negro Americans.* Atlanta: Atlanta Univ. Press, 1907.

—————. *The Negro American Family.* Atlanta: Atlanta Univ. Press, 1908.

—————. *The Negro in Business.* Atlanta: Atlanta Univ. Press, 1899.

Du Bois, W. E. B., and August G. Dill, eds. *The College-Bred Negro American.* Atlanta: Atlanta Univ. Press, 1910.

Dun, R. G., & Co., comp. *The Mercantile Agency Reference Book (and Key) Containing Ratings on the Merchants, Manufacturers, and Traders Generally, Throughout the United States and Canada.* New York, 1870–1915. Bound volumes in Library of Congress, Washington DC.

Edmonds, Helen. *The Negro and Fusion Politics in North Carolina, 1894–1901.* Chapel Hill: Univ. of North Carolina Press, 1951.

Elkins, Stanley M. *Slavery: A Problem of American Institutional and Intellectual Life.* Chicago: Univ. of Chicago Press, 1959.

Fogel, Robert W., and Stanley L. Engerman. *Time on the Cross: The Economics of American Negro Slavery.* Boston: Little, Brown, 1974.

Franklin, John Hope. *The Free Negro in North Carolina, 1790–1860.* Chapel Hill: Univ. of North Carolina Press, 1943.

Frazier, E. Franklin. *The Negro Family in the United States*. Chicago: Univ. of Chicago Press, 1939.

Fuller, Thomas. *Twenty Years in Public Life, 1890–1910*. Nashville: National Baptist Publishing Board, 1910.

Gatewood, Willard B. *Aristocrats of Color: The Black Elite, 1880–1920*. Bloomington: Indiana Univ. Press, 1990.

Genovese, Eugene D. *Roll Jordan Roll: Afro-American Slaves in the Making of the Modern World*. New York: Pantheon, 1974.

Greenwood, Janette Thomas. *Bittersweet Legacy: The Black and White "Better Classes" in Charlotte, 1850–1910*. Chapel Hill: Univ. of North Carolina Press, 1994.

Gutman, Herbert F. *The Black Family in Slavery and Freedom, 1750–1925*. New York: Pantheon, 1976.

Haley, John H. *Charles N. Hunter and Race Relations in North Carolina*. Chapel Hill: Univ. of North Carolina Press, 1987.

Hamilton, J. G. de Roulhac. *Reconstruction in North Carolina*. New York: Columbia Univ. Press, 1914.

Harris, Abram L. *The Negro as Capitalist: A Study of Banking and Business among American Negroes*. College Park MD: McGrath, 1936.

Higgs, Robert. *Competition and Coercion: Blacks in the American Economy, 1865–1914*. Cambridge: Cambridge Univ. Press, 1977.

Holt, Thomas. *Black over White: Negro Political Leadership in South Carolina during Reconstruction*. Urbana: Univ. of Illinois Press, 1977.

Johnson, Michael P., and James L. Roark. *Black Masters: A Free Family of Color in the Old South*. New York: W. W. Norton, 1984.

Kennedy, William J., Jr. *The North Carolina Mutual Story: A Symbol of Progress, 1898–1970*. Durham: North Carolina Mutual Life Insurance Company, 1970.

Kenzer, Robert C. *Kinship and Neighborhood in a Southern Community: Orange County, North Carolina, 1849–1881*. Knoxville: Univ. of Tennessee Press, 1987.

Logan, Frenise A. *The Negro in North Carolina, 1876–1894*. Chapel Hill: Univ. of North Carolina Press, 1964.

Meier, August. *Negro Thought in America, 1880–1915: Race Ideologies in the Age of Booker T. Washington*. Ann Arbor: Univ. of Michigan Press, 1963.

Montgomery, Lizzie Wilson. *Sketches of Old Warrenton, North Carolina: Traditions and Reminiscences of the Town and People Who Made It*. Raleigh: Edwards & Broughton, 1924.

Muraskin, William A. *Middle-Class Blacks in a White Society: Prince Hall Freemasonry in America*. Berkeley: Univ. of California Press, 1975.

Murray, Pauli. *Proud Shoes: The Story of an American Family*. New York: Harper & Row, 1956.

Norris, James D. *R. G. Dun & Co., 1841–1900: The Development of Credit-Reporting in the Nineteenth Century*. Westport CT: Greenwood, 1978.

Penn, I. Garland. *The Afro-American Press and Its Editors.* Springfield MA: Wiley, 1891.

Powell, William S. *Higher Education in North Carolina.* Raleigh: North Carolina State Department of Archives and History, 1964.

————. *North Carolina through Four Centuries.* Chapel Hill: Univ. of North Carolina Press, 1989.

————, ed. *Dictionary of North Carolina Biography.* 5 vols. to date. Chapel Hill: Univ. of North Carolina Press, 1979–.

Prather, Leon H. *We Have Taken a City.* Cranbury NJ: Associated Universities Presses, 1984.

Quick, W. H. *Negro Stars in All Ages of the World.* Rockingham NC: privately published, 1897.

Rabinowitz, Howard. *Race Relations in the Urban South, 1865–1890.* New York: Oxford Univ. Press, 1978.

Ransom, Roger, and Richard Sutch. *One Kind of Freedom: The Economic Consequences of Emancipation.* Cambridge: Cambridge Univ. Press, 1977.

Raper, Arthur F. *Preface to Peasantry: A Tale of Two Black Belt Counties.* Chapel Hill: Univ. of North Carolina Press, 1936.

Reuter Edward Byron. *The Mulatto in the United States.* New York: Negro Universities Press, 1918.

Richardson, Clement, ed. *The National Encyclopedia of the Colored Race.* Montgomery AL: National Publishing, 1919.

Ross, Elizabeth, and Ray King, comps. *Marriage Records of Johnston County, North Carolina, 1867–1880.* N.p.: privately published, 1986.

Savage, W. Sherman. *Blacks in the West.* Westport CT: Greenwood, 1976.

Schweninger, Loren. *Black Property Owners in the South, 1790–1915.* Urbana: Univ. of Illinois Press, 1990.

————, ed. *From Tennessee Slave to St. Louis Entrepreneur: The Autobiography of James Thomas.* Columbia: Univ. of Missouri Press, 1984.

Sitterson, Joseph Carlyle. *The Secession Movement in North Carolina.* Chapel Hill: Univ. of North Carolina Press, 1939.

Stampp, Kenneth M. *The Peculiar Institution: Slavery in the Ante-Bellum South.* New York: Alfred A. Knopf, 1956.

Walker, Juliet E. K. *Free Frank: A Black Pioneer on the Antebellum Frontier.* Lexington: Univ. Press of Kentucky, 1983.

Washington, Booker T. *The Negro in Business.* Chicago: Hartel, Jenkins,, 1907.

Weare, Walter B. *Black Business in the New South: A Social History of the North Carolina Mutual Life Insurance Company.* Urbana: Univ. of Illinois Press, 1973.

Wellman, Manly Wade. *The County of Warren, North Carolina, 1586–1917.* Chapel Hill: Univ. of North Carolina Press, 1959.

White, Barnetta McGhee. *In Search of Kith and Kin: The History of a Southern Black Family.* Baltimore: Gateway, 1986.

Wier, Sadye H., and John F. Marszalek. *A Black Businessman in White Mississippi, 1886–1974.* Oxford: Univ. Press of Mississippi, 1977.

Williams, Loretta J. *Black Freemasonry and Middle Class Realities.* Columbia: Univ. of Missouri Press, 1980.

Wrenn, Tony P. *Wilmington, North Carolina: An Architectural and Historical Portrait.* Charlottesville: Univ. Press of Virginia, 1984.

Articles and Chapters

Banks, Enoch Martin. "The Economics of Land Tenure in Georgia." *Studies in History, Economics, and Public Laws* 23 (1905): 1–142.

Crow, Jeffrey J. "An Apartheid for the South: Clarence Poe's Crusade for Rural Segregation." In *Race, Class, and Politics in Southern History: Essays in Honor of Robert F. Durden,* ed. Jeffrey J. Crow et al., 216–59. Baton Rouge: Louisiana State Univ. Press, 1989.

Engerrand, Steven W. "Black and Mulatto Mobility and Stability in Dallas, Texas, 1880–1910." *Phylon* 39 (fall 1978): 203–15.

Harmon, J. H., Jr. "The Negro as a Local Businessman." *Journal of Negro History* 14 (April 1929): 116–55.

Hershberg, Theodore, and Henry Williams. "Mulattoes and Blacks: Intra-Group Color Differences and Social Stratification in Nineteenth Century Philadelphia." In *Philadelphia: Work, Space, Family, and Group Experience in the Nineteenth Century,* ed. Theodore Hershberg, 392–434. New York: Oxford Univ. Press, 1981.

Higgs, Robert. "Accumulation of Property by Southern Blacks before World War I." *American Economic Review* 72 (September 1982): 725–37.

———. "Accumulation of Property by Southern Blacks before World War I: Reply." *American Economic Review* 74 (September 1984): 771–81.

———. "Participation of Blacks and Immigrants in the American Merchant Class, 1890–1910." *Explorations in Economic History* 13 (April 1976): 153–64.

Holt, Sharon Ann. "Making Freedom Pay: Freedpeople Working for Themselves, North Carolina, 1865–1900." *Journal of Southern History* 60 (May 1994): 229–62.

Hopkins, Richard J. "Occupational and Geographic Mobility in Atlanta, 1870–1896." *Journal of Southern History* 34 (May 1968): 200–213.

Kenzer, Robert C. "The Black Business Community in Post Civil War Virginia." *Southern Studies* 4 (fall 1993): 229–52.

———. "The Black Businessman in the Postwar South: North Carolina, 1865–1880." *Business History Review* 63 (spring 1989): 61–87.

———. "Black Businessmen in Post–Civil War Tennessee." *Journal of East Tennessee History* 66 (1994): 59–80.

———. "Credit Ratings of Georgia Black Businessmen, 1865–1880." *Georgia Historical Quarterly* 79 (summer 1995): 425–40.

Kolchin, Peter. "American Historians and Antebellum Southern Slavery, 1959–1984." In *A Master's Due: Essays in Honor of David Herbert Donald,* ed.

William J. Cooper et al., 87–111. Baton Rouge: Louisiana State Univ. Press, 1985.

Logan, Frenise A. "The Colored Industrial Association of North Carolina and Its Fair of 1886." *North Carolina Historical Review* 34 (January 1957): 58–67.

————. "The Economic Status of the Town Negro in Post-Reconstruction North Carolina." *North Carolina Historical Review* 35 (October 1958): 448–60.

Margo, Robert. "Accumulation of Property by Southern Blacks before World War I: Comment and Further Evidence." *American Economic Review* 74 (September 1984): 768–76.

Mobley, Joe. "In the Shadow of White Society: Princeville, a Black Town in North Carolina, 1865–1915." *North Carolina Historical Review* 63 (July 1986): 340–84.

Morton, Patricia. "From Visible Man to 'New People': The Recent Discovery of American Mulattoes." *Phylon* 46 (summer 1985): 106–22.

Walker, Juliet E. K. "Racism, Slavery, and Free Enterprise: Black Entrepreneurship in the United States before the Civil War." *Business History Review* 60 (autumn 1986): 343–82.

Woodman, Harold D. "Economic Reconstruction and the Rise of the New South, 1865–1900." In *Interpreting Southern History: Historiographical Essays in Honor of Sanford W. Higginbotham,* ed. John B. Boles and Evelyn Thomas Nolen, 254–307. Baton Rouge: Louisiana State Univ. Press, 1987.

————. "Sequel to Slavery: A New History of the Postwar South." *Journal of Southern History* 42 (November 1977): 523–54.

Worthman, Paul B. "Working Class Mobility in Birmingham, Alabama, 1880–1914." In *Anonymous Americans: Explorations in Nineteenth-Century Social History,* ed. Tamara K. Hareven, 172–213. Englewood Cliffs, NJ: Prentice-Hall, 1971.

Dissertations, Theses, and Unpublished Papers

Burgess, Allen Edward. "Tar Heel Blacks and the New South Dream: The Coleman Manufacturing Company, 1896–1904." Ph.D. diss., Duke University, 1977.

Holt, Sharon Ann. "A Time to Plant: The Economic Lives of Freedpeople in Granville County, North Carolina, 1865–1900." Ph.D. diss., University of Pennsylvania, 1991.

Nowaczyk, Elaine. "The North Carolina Negro in Politics." M.A. thesis, University of North Carolina, 1958.

Robinson, Armstead L. "A 'New Birth of Freedom': Reflections on the 375th Anniversary of the African Arrival in Virginia." Paper presented at Hampton University, 19 August 1994.

Index

as private incorporation bill sponsors, 96, 154 n.29; after Reconstruction, 90–96; wealth and prominence in business, 89–90. *See also names of individual legislators*

Leonard Medical School (of Shaw University), 82, 114, 122, 123, 124, 159 n.42

Lincoln University, 92, 114, 119

liquor trade. *See under* local officeholders

Livingstone College, 114, 116, 120, 121, 122

local (black county and municipal) officeholders, 96; aid black business, 99; antebellum status of, 96; and liquor trade, 99–100, 155 n.43; and property ownership, 96, 154 n.31. *See also names of individual local black officeholders*

Logan, Frenise A., 142 n.3

Lomax, Thomas, 70

Louisbourg, 59

Lowe, Chas. E., & Co., 54

Lowrey, James A., 41, 70, 98, 107

Lowrey, Wiley, 71, 107

Mandle, Jay R., 136 n.9

marriage and family (black), 7, 109–13; and antebellum status, 109–11, 156 n.4; and economic status, 109–13; intermarriage of blacks and mulattoes, 110–11

Masons (Prince Hall Freemasonry), 6, 69–75; assist black enterprise, 73; benevolence and charitable activities of, 73–74; and credit-rated firms, 70, 148 n.10; dues, 72; emergency aid for members, 73–74; lodge and membership growth, 69; lodges as black cultural centers, 73; occupations of members, 70; political participa-

tion, 69–79, 148 n.5; property management experience, 72–73; real estate ownership of, 70, 71, 72; turnover of members, 71, 149 n.13. *See also names of individual lodges*

Mayo, Cuffie, 87

Mayzek, John, 43

McCullers, Bythan, 19

McDonald, Mustaphor, 11

McGhee, Robert and Caroline (and their descendants), 27–32

Mebane, George Allen, xiv, 1–4, 8

Mechanics and Farmers Bank (of Durham), 81–83, 108, 124; financial success and resources, 82, 151 n.60; leaders, 81–82

Meier, August, 7

Mercantile Agency Reference Book, 142 n.3

Merrick, Edward, 82, 124

Merrick, John, 76, 81–82, 83, 84

Method, 67, 106

Milton, 49, 51

Montauk Social League, 113–14

Moore, A., 54

Moore, Dr. Aaron McDuffie, 81, 82, 83

Moore, Willis P., 101

Morganton, 54

Mount Lebanon Lodge (Tarboro), 60, 73

Mount Moriah Lodge (South Mills), 72

Mutual Aid Banking Co. (of New Bern), 80, 81, 151 n.52

Nash, William, 73

National Negro Business League, 4, 6, 67, 83–85; dues, 84, 152 n.67; link to black business, 83, 152 n.65; membership in North Carolina, 83; size of communities with charters, 83; stresses achieve-

Carter G. Woodson Institute Series in Black Studies

Michael Plunkett
Afro-American Sources in Virginia: A Guide to Manuscripts

Sally Belfrage
Freedom Summer

Armstead L. Robinson and Patricia Sullivan, eds.
New Directions in Civil Rights Studies

Leroy Vail and Landeg White
Power and the Praise Poem: Southern African Voices in History

Robert A. Pratt
The Color of Their Skin: Education and Race in Richmond, Virginia, 1954–89

Ira Berlin and Philip D. Morgan, eds.
Cultivation and Culture: Labor and the Shaping of Slave Life in the Americas

Gerald Horne
Fire This Time: The Watts Uprising and the 1960s

Sam C. Nolutshungu
Limits of Anarchy: Intervention and State Formation in Chad

Jeannie M. Whayne
A New Plantation South: Land, Labor, and Federal Favor in Twentieth-Century Arkansas

Patience Essah
A House Divided: Slavery and Emancipation in Delaware, 1638–1865

Tommy L. Bogger
Free Blacks in Norfolk, Virginia, 1790–1860: The Darker Side of Freedom

Robert C. Kenzer
Enterprising Southerners: Black Economic Success in North Carolina, 1865–1915